FREEDOM

FREEDOM

Maurice Cranston

BASIC BOOKS, INC., PUBLISHERS

New York

First published 1953
Second edition 1954
Third edition © Maurice Cranston 1967
Library of Congress Catalog Card Number: 68–20961
Printed in the United States of America

CONTENTS

Introduction   vii
Note to Revised Edition   vii

Part 1

THE MEANING OF FREEDOM

1. Words   3
2. Meanings   11
3. Theories   17
4. Definitions   24
5. Persuasion   33

Part 2

THE AMBIGUITY OF LIBERALISM

1. English Liberalism   47
2. French Liberalism   58
3. German Liberalism   64
4. American Liberalism   70

Part 3

THE FREEDOM OF THE WILL

1. Is there a Problem of the Will?   81
2. Solutions   95
3. Ethics   106
4. Prediction   113

Summary   123
Further Reading   125
Index of Proper Names   129

INTRODUCTION

This book is about the meaning of freedom. It begins, but it does not end, with linguistic analysis. Wittgenstein said: 'The purpose of philosophy is clarification.' Although I disagree that such is the *only* purpose of philosophy I am persuaded that it is the first.

What I have to say may possibly help students confronted with the perennial examination question on *freedom*. I should like equally to interest more general readers, especially those who have felt, as I have felt, bewildered or dissatisfied by the vast literature of this subject, but who still believe that there is something yet to be said. I do not aspire with this book to say that thing worth saying, but simply to contribute 'some notes towards' it.

I have divided the book into three parts. The first deals with points of language and philosophy. The second is a short scrutiny of liberalism, as a political doctrine based on a principle of liberty; the third deals with the problem of the freedom of the will.

Some of the paragraphs printed here have appeared in articles of mine in *World Review*, *Philosophy* and *The Hibbert Journal* and in talks I have given on the Third Programme of the BBC. Part 1 and Part 3 reproduce the arguments of a thesis for which I received the Oxford degree of B.Litt.

I wish to acknowledge the help of several people who have discussed my subject with me, or who have read and criticized the manuscript. They include the following (whom I name without suggesting that they in any way agree with me): Professor Sir Karl R. Popper, the late Professor John Hartland-Swann, Professor W. D. Falk, Professor Richard Peters, Mr Peter Alexander, Professor J. W. N. Watkins and Mr Richard Robinson.

NOTE TO REVISED EDITION

This edition contains a number of minor corrections which have been suggested to me by reviewers and other readers. I have not altered the substance of the argument, although my views have changed in some respects since I wrote the original text. I have added to this edition a bibliography which includes books and papers published since the earlier editions of this book appeared.

Part 1

THE MEANING OF FREEDOM

I

WORDS

Consider how much—or rather how little—you say if you say you are
free. Imagine a meeting with a stranger. You know nothing about him
or his predicament. He approaches you and says: 'I am free.' You are
baffled. Has he just escaped from prison, from his debts, from his wife,
from his sins? He has told you he is free, but he has not told you what he
is free *from*. He has confided remarkably little.

Yet if the stranger had said: 'I am hungry', you would have known
only too well what he meant. In its structure the sentence 'I am free'
looks like the sentence 'I am hungry'. That resemblance is deceptive.
For whereas 'I am hungry' has one meaning, 'I am free' might have any
one of a vast range of possible meanings. If we are to know which of
those innumerable possibilities is intended, we must know what it is
that a man who says he is free, is free from. He must name a constraint,
impediment or burden.[1]

Suppose I say 'This bird was in a cage, but now it is free'; then I
shall have given meaning to the words 'it is free' by saying that it *was*
in a cage. I have said it is free from its former captivity: I have said
what it is free from. Sometimes the situation in which the words are
spoken is such that the impediment, constraint or burden need not be
named because that factor is already understood. A divorce court judge
knows when a petitioner speaks of her 'freedom', that she means her
freedom from the matrimonial tie. But the context does not always
enlighten. The word '*libre*' on the door of a *cabinet* in France means
'unoccupied': the word 'free' on a similar door in England means 'no
charge for admission'.

There is a story of a German pupil of Martin Heidegger having proclaimed in all solemnity that he was *resolved*. He had learned from his
master the importance of 'the resolve'. But he did not know what he
was resolved to do. '*Ich bin entschlossen, ich weiss nur nicht wozu!*' It

---

[1] Compare the word 'free' with the word 'prepared'. If I say 'I am prepared',
you will not learn much unless you know what I am prepared for—war, the bath,
the Day of Judgment or whatever it may be.

3

would be no less absurd for a man to say he was *free* and not to know from what.

§

Should we have considered being free *to* rather than being free *from*? Such an approach might attract a mind which is anxious to emphasize the positive. It is unlikely, however, to lead very far.

I may say 'I am free to dine with you this evening' or 'I am free to leave London tomorrow'. I mean, when I use these words, that I am free *from* anything that would prevent my doing what is mentioned. 'I am free to dine with you this evening' is another way of saying 'I am free from any sort of engagement or impediment that might have stood in the way of my dining with you this evening'. It is shorter, but it is not more 'positive'.

No one thinks a set of circumstances constraining unless he wants to do something which those circumstances prevent or hinder. The law which forbids the importation of parrots into the United Kingdom is not felt as a constraint or impediment by people who have no desire to import parrots into the United Kingdom. If we have no desire to do things, we should hardly know the meaning of constraint.

Constraints stand opposed to our desires; freedom stands opposed to constraints. A reason for liking freedom is that we do not like constraints. Nor do we like the other things with which we contrast our freedom. We speak of being free from *burdens*—such as debts and responsibilities—which we tend to dislike. We speak of being free from *nuisances*—such as rats and the noise of other people's parties. A complication arises from the fact, which we must later examine, that some burdens (duties, responsibilities), even some constraints *are* liked. But generally the presence of constraints, impediments and burdens is unwelcome. It is when they are absent, and we rejoice, that we say we are free.

We do not speak of ourselves as being free from something we should welcome. We hear of 'a tax-free investment'. Who has ever heard of a 'dividend-free investment'?

Compare the three phrases: 'to be without', 'to lack' and 'to be free from'. We use the word 'lack' when we speak of things we are without and *regret* we are without. 'I lack Spanish', 'I lack powers of concentration'. We use the expression 'free from' when we speak of those things we are without and *are glad* we are without. 'My throat is free from infection', 'The house is free from damp'. We use the words

'without' or 'has not', when we are indifferent. I say 'John Locke died
without issue', because I am neither pleased about that fact nor sorry.

§

Our habit of saying we are free when we are without something we
are glad to be without, might prompt us to agree with writers who
tell us that freedom is good. I think we should not agree too readily.
For there is no *one* freedom but many freedoms; and they are as
various as are constraints, impediments and burdens.

Furthermore, if once a man agrees, in conversation with philosophers
and politicians, that freedom is good without being quite clear what he
means by 'freedom', he is likely to find himself being *told* what 'freedom' means, and forced to agree that *that* is good.

Many philosophers and politicians have written about 'freedom' as
if it were a word like 'immortality' or 'monarchy' or 'popery'; something both lofty and difficult to understand, but nevertheless positive
and uniquely descriptive. Having allowed themselves the privilege of
using the word 'free' without naming the constraint, impediment or
burden to which it stands opposed, such writers have often come to
assume that there is something vulgar about associating the word
'free' with any particular constraining factor. Aristotle[1] says that if
freedom means the absence of constraint, it points to a state of affairs
in which 'each man lives as he likes', a thought from which Aristotle
recoils. Heidegger does not speak for himself alone when he says:
'Freedom is not what common sense is content to let pass under that
name.'[2] He speaks for a long line of philosophers who have felt with
Aristotle that what common sense is content with is a 'mean conception
of liberty'.[3]

There is said to have been in Nashville, Tennessee, a Negro gentleman whose name was Marquis Of. Visitors would sometimes ask him
'Marquis of what?' 'Just "Marquis Of" ' he would say. If they continued to look puzzled, he would explain: 'In Nashville "Of" is a
respected family name. My first name is Marquis, and nobody in
Nashville would ever think of asking me "Marquis of *what?*" '

Some readers of philosophical and political books are like those
people of Nashville, Tennessee. They are so used to the name of 'freedom' that they would never think of asking 'freedom *from what?*' It

[1] *Politics*, V, ix, § 15, 16.
[2] *Existence and Being* (London, 1949), p. 334.
[3] Aristotle, *Politics, loc. cit.*

may even seem ill-mannered to suggest that it should ever be done. I
believe that it should always be done.

§

Lord Acton proposed to write a history of mankind in terms of its
struggle towards freedom. Rousseau opened his treatise on *The Social
Contract* with the famous words: 'Man was born free, and he is every-
where in chains.' If the word 'free' had unique descriptive meaning,
Acton and Rousseau would have been in conflict here over a matter of
fact, Acton holding that men were becoming more free than they once
were, Rousseau that they had become less free. Since the word 'free'
has not such uniquely descriptive meaning, it does not follow that
Acton and Rousseau were in conflict on any matter of fact.

They were at variance in what they understood by 'freedom'. Acton
seems to have meant by 'freedom'—freedom from the constraints of
nature, freedom from disease and hunger and insecurity and ignorance
and superstition. Freedom from these constraints I will call the
Progressive image of freedom.

When Rousseau spoke of 'freedom' in this context, he usually
meant freedom from the constraints of advanced political institutions
of modern European civilization. Freedom from such constraints is
promoted by a return to more primitive and natural ways of living. I
will call this the *Romantic*[1] image of freedom.

The Progressive and the Romantic are thus both employing the
same word 'freedom', but they are asking for different things. They are
demanding freedom from different constraints. What is more, each is
asking for a freedom which experience teaches us can only be pur-
chased at the price of precisely that freedom which the other cherishes.
Freedom from the constraints of nature (the Progressive demand) has
been achieved, where it has been achieved, in exchange for the constraints of advanced political institutions—policemen, compulsory

---

[1] The *Progressive* image of freedom does not underlie all Acton's teaching; nor
was the *Romantic* image the only one held by Rousseau. Each offers what appears
to be a definition of 'freedom' as follows:

(*a*) Lord Acton (*History of Freedom*, London, 1907, p. 3) says: 'By liberty I
mean the assurance that every man shall be protected in doing what he believes
to be his duty against the influences of authority and majorities, custom and
opinion.'

(*b*) Rousseau (*Du Contrat Social*, I, 8): 'L'impulsion du seul appétit est esclavage,
et l'obéissance à la loi qu'on s'est prescrite est liberté.' Rousseau adds, however, the
note: 'le sens philosophique du mot *liberté* n'est pas ici de mon sujet.'

education and the Welfare State. Where the constraints of advanced political institutions have been removed, as they were removed from the Negroes who left the United States for Liberia, servitude to nature and the hardships of a primitive society have replaced the earlier servitude to the institutions of the modern state.

The Progressive looks forward. The more civilized and industrialized a society, the more freedom (freedom, that is from the constraints of nature) he discerns. The industrial revolution, the progress of science, the spread of education are all seen as liberating forces. The Progressive tends to admire such societies as England and the U.S.A.

The Romantic, on the other hand, looks backward. If there is servitude to nature, where there are no advanced political institutions, such servitude, he argues, is at least *natural*. The servitude to political institutions which follows from the existence of the modern state is artificial, and for that reason evil. The Romantic admires communities like the ancient Swiss cantons of Glarus and Appenzell, where men kept a primitive democracy alive in modern times, and lived close to the soil, unlettered and poor, but without political masters.

The conflict here is a simple one. The state of affairs the Progressive sees as servitude, the Romantic calls freedom, and that which the Romantic sees as servitude the Progressive calls freedom. There is a quarrel here in which the opposing principles are both given the same name. It is freedom *versus* freedom, and the surprising thing is that we are able to make anything at all of their encounter. Imagine hearing a wireless commentary on a boxing match between those celebrated pugilists of the past who shared the name of Johnson. How perplexing it would be if the commentator spoke of both of them as 'Johnson'. But no commentator would be so foolish. The accent would be on *James* and *John* and not on Johnson. There is a lesson here for philosophers and politicians and all who write and talk about freedom.

§

It may be said that so far as *political* (as distinct from philosophical) controversies go, the word 'freedom' is generally understood precisely because the constraining factor from which that freedom is claimed is generally understood.

At the time of the Roman kings, for example, 'freedom' was unequivocal. It meant freedom from the rule of the kings. But when that rule ended, when freedom (in that sense) was achieved, 'freedom' ceased to be unequivocal. With the abolition of the Roman monarchy, as Dr Wirszubski has pointed out,[1] the Romans began to shift the reference of the word '*libertas*' to something positive. '*Libertas*' meant no longer the absence of monarchy, but a concept of popular government embodied in the republican constitution of the commonwealth. The *res publica populi Romani Quiritium* was the embodiment of *libertas populi Romani*, just as *civitas Romana* was the embodiment of *libertas civis Romani*. However, as Dr Wirszubski explains, the Roman constitution was not a constant. The word '*libertas*', associated with the republican constitution during the Republican period, was later associated with the Principate, in spite of the radical changes in the nature of the Principate during the first century A.D.

The example of Rome shows that the word '*libertas*' had one accepted meaning only so long as it stood opposed to one particular constraint to which *everyone knew* it stood opposed. Once that state of affairs ended, the word '*libertas*' floated unanchored on the tides of demagogy.

The lesson of Rome is the lesson of history generally. The word 'liberty' has its least ambiguity in political use in times of centralized oppression. That is because the constraint or burden from which liberty is sought is clearly understood. In Europe between 1815 and 1848 a man who proclaimed liberty would be understood to mean liberty from the kings and emperors who then occupied the thrones of Europe. There was no doubt about what Byron meant when he sang:

> Yet Freedom, yet, thy banner torn but flying,
> Streams like the thunderstorm *against* the wind.[2]

This is because there was no doubt about what Byron wanted freedom *from*. When he told how he mused at Marathon and 'dream'd that Greece might still be free'[3] he could not have been thought to mean anything but 'free from Turkish rule'.

In France, at the end of the eighteenth century, the call for freedom was a call for freedom from despotic Bourbon rule, as in England during the first half of the seventeenth century the call for freedom had been a call for freedom from despotic Stuart rule.

The words 'freedom' and 'liberty' can be clearly understood in political manifestos only in so far as they are recognized as having definite reference to some such specific constraint. The meaning is most

[1] *Libertas*, by C. Wirszubski (Cambridge, 1952).
[2] *Childe Harold*, IV. xcviii.
[3] *Don Juan*, III. lxxxvi.

clear when those in authority admit that they stand opposed to liberty. Such admissions have rarely been made anywhere in the world; in England and America, perhaps never.

Charles the First is reported to have said from the scaffold on 30 January 1649:[1]

> For the People; and truly I desire their Liberty and Freedom as much as anybody whomsoever; but I must tell you, that Liberty and Freedom consist in having of Government, and those laws by which their Life and their Goods may be most their own. It is not having a share in Government, sir; that is nothing pertaining to them.

This seems to be a royal definition of the word 'freedom', or to be more exact, a redefinition. And it is clear what effect the royal utterance was designed to achieve. By proclaiming himself in favour of freedom (redefined) the King stole the colours of the rebels; or rather he stole the shorthand sign 'freedom' which they had made to stand for 'freedom from Stuart rule' and made that sign stand instead for 'freedom from anarchy'.

The proper rejoinder would have been to call for the full version of all such abbreviated slogans. That rejoinder did not come. The call for freedom lost its anchorage again. It came to be used, as so often before and since, to mean different and even contrary principles in the minds of different people.

America in the 1860s provides an instructive example. Both belligerents in the Civil War said that they were fighting for freedom. Some people may have thought because of this, that one side or the other was lying. In fact, each side was making an incomplete pronouncement. Both, so far as they went, were speaking the truth. The South could truly claim that it was fighting for the freedom of State governments from Federal interference; the North could truly claim that it was fighting, among other things, to free the Negroes of the South from slavery. Abraham Lincoln began to detect what was happening when he said in a speech at Baltimore in 1864: 'The world has never had a good definition of the word "liberty" . . . in using the same word, we do not mean the same thing.'[2]

[1] *The Works of King Charles* (London, 1662), p. 454.
[2] Lincoln was unjust when he went on to suggest that 'liberty' for his own side in the war meant 'liberty for each man to do as he pleases with himself' while for his enemies the word meant 'liberty for some men to do as they please with other men'. His enemies could truly claim that they used the word 'liberty' to mean 'liberty for each American State to rule itself as it pleases'.

Another, no less thoughtful President, Franklin D. Roosevelt, is remarkable among the statesmen of history in having seen that it is not enough to speak of 'freedom' unless one explains what one wishes to be free from or free for. Thus, when he proclaimed as the goals of Allied policy in the Second World War, *four* freedoms—freedom from fear, freedom from want, freedom of worship and freedom of speech— Roosevelt made his programme *meaningful*. It was perhaps an unrealistic, Utopian programme, but at least it could be understood.

§

When you talk of freedom, you cannot be sure of making your meaning clear by putting an adjective in front of the substantive. We often hear, for example, of 'economic freedom' and 'religious freedom'. Neither is unambiguous.

The expression 'economic freedom' has at least two meanings in current use. Sometimes the expression is used to denote what is also called a 'free economic system'—an economic system free from the control of the State. Sometimes it is used to denote the freedom of the individual from economic hardship.

In the political writings of today both conservatives and socialists advocate 'economic freedom'. Conservatives, when they speak of 'economic freedom', usually mean 'the freedom of the national economy from the controls of the State'. Socialists usually mean 'freedom from economic hardship'.

What makes this ambiguity particularly unfortunate is that the 'economic freedom' recommended by the socialists is held by them to be possible only at the expense of 'economic freedom' in the sense in which it is recommended by conservatives. Thus the political controversies of the present day disclose a paradox analogous to the case where 'freedom' recommended by the Romantic and Progressive respectively turned out to be purchasable in either sense only at the expense of 'freedom' in the other.

Likewise we find the expression 'religious freedom' used sometimes to mean 'freedom (from state interference) for religious institutions', and at others to mean 'freedom (for individuals) *from* religious institutions'. (People who want freedom *from* religious institutions often look to State interference to secure it.)

An adjective in front of 'freedom' can be depended on to eliminate equivocation only if it says what that freedom is freedom from or freedom for.

2

MEANINGS

Sometimes we say we *feel free*. A constraint or burden has passed from us, and for some little while afterwards (rarely for very long) we have a sense of relief, even exhilaration, which we connect with our release[1] from that particular constraint, impediment or burden. Examples of several sorts suggest themselves.

1. You have a chance to *indulge* your desires and whims without the usual bar of authority or inhibition. You feel free.
2. You *master* one of your habitual weaknesses; smoking, it may be, or staying late in bed. You feel free.
3. You experience a *change* of bondage. You are drafted into the army. You feel free (free, that is, from the constraints peculiar to civilian life). You are discharged from the army. You feel free (free from the constraints peculiar to military life).

The examples illustrate a simple point. The constraints of life are of many kinds. They come and go: and when they go we say we feel *freed* of them. The things we like are just as various. When they go we feel *deprived* of them. Sometimes we regard something as a constraint, and thus feel freed when it goes, but later on begin to wish we had it again; at that point we cease to say we are *free* of it, and begin instead to *miss* it, to feel the *loss* of it.

'Freedom' and 'liberty' are examples of what philosophers of the vernacular call *hurrah*-words. To say 'I am free from debts, is to say 'I am without debts, hurrah!' Correspondingly, 'lack' might be called an *alas*-word. To say 'I lack Spanish' is to say 'I am without Spanish, alas!' Each sentence announces the facts and at the same time expresses your feelings about the facts, your attitude towards them.

Do 'freedom' and 'liberty' invariably indicate approval? Many

---

[1] 'Release' is a laudatory word like 'free', as an English Minister realized when he gave the following Answer to a Question in the House of Commons:

Question: 'Is it true that workers have been dismissed?'
Answer: 'No Sir; labour has been released.'

Victorians spoke of 'free-love' and 'free-thought' without approving of either. In the twentieth century many have turned against 'free-trade' and 'free enterprise'. Even so, it seems that although people who do not like the institutions *use* the names, those names were introduced by people who did like them.

Notice, too, that critics of free-love, for example, have often said it is not *really* free, but licentious. 'Licence they mean when they cry liberty,' said Milton, claiming that only the good could be free.[1]

'Licence' is a pejorative word or what is sometimes called a *boo*-word. Milton, who disliked political constraints, would say when political constraints were absent: 'This is liberty.' With that word he both announced the absence of constraint and expressed his pleasure or approval. But since Milton favoured moral constraints, he would say when moral constraints were absent: 'This is licence.' With that word he both announced the absence of constraint and expressed his displeasure or disapproval.

§

We are dealing now with what may be called the *extra-descriptive* aspects of language, the functions words fulfil besides that of conveying information. We have seen that words express feelings and attitudes. They can also generate feelings. If this were not so, we should not enjoy poetry. Part of the poet's task is to express his feelings and convey them to us; he does not write primarily to communicate information, though he will probably communicate *some* information. A scientific writer, on the other hand, tries to communicate information and not to generate feelings. Between the poet and the scientist is the ordinary prose writer and speaker who uses language in no single way, but to inform and to express and to evoke, among other purposes.

These observations recall not only the work of Wittgenstein, but that of I. A. Richards,[2] who made the study of the emotive aspects of language popular. I myself disagree with Richards on several grounds. I do not believe that all words must be *either* emotive or descriptive

---

[1] I quote from Milton's *Sonnets* (No. xii):

'Licence they mean when they cry liberty
For who loves that must first be good and wise.'

Again, in *The Tenure of Kings and Magistrates*, Milton says: 'None can love freedom heartily but good men; the rest love not freedom but licence.'

[2] I refer here to Richards's early work: *The Meaning of Meaning* (1923), *The Principles of Literary Criticism* (1925), *Science and Poetry* (1926).

but that almost every word has something of both sorts of meaning. The dearth of wholly non-emotive language has driven scientists to work with symbols; and one of the reasons why social scientists like Max Weber have failed to produce a value-free sociology is that a large proportion of the words they use have evaluation built into them.

Secondly, Richards encouraged the belief that descriptive or scientific language was always desirable, and emotive language undesirable. Hence in the United States, where Richards's influence has been greatest, the word 'emotive' has itself become an emotive word— a *boo*-word.

When Charles L. Stevenson adapted Richards's technique to the study of ethics, he stripped it of much of its primitive extremism,[1] and there is still much to be learned from his book *Ethics and Language*.

In speaking of the emotive meaning of a word, I intend only to say that the descriptive aspects of a word's meaning do not exhaust the whole of its meaning. The emotive aspects are no less important. Stevenson speaks of the difficulty of finding a clear-cut basis for distinguishing these aspects. I suspect there is no clear-cut basis to be found. A second problem—rightly, perhaps, the first—is to give a satisfactory analysis of meaning itself.

Stevenson works on a psychological theory of meaning.[2] A sign, on this view, has meaning for a hearer when it has a disposition or (as Stevenson chose later to call it) a tendency to cause the hearer to respond in a regular way to other similar stimuli. It is not necessary that this pragmatic meaning of a sign shall be identified with any single response of the hearer. What matters is that the reception of the sign shall induce a fixed pattern of response. Then, varying with other circumstances, the sign will have meaning. To say that a sign causes a disposition to respond is merely to indicate the modified routine of behaviour of which it is the precipitating cause. When the correlated responses are (a) cognitive in nature, the sign has *descriptive* meaning. When the responses evoked by the sign are (b) a range of emotions, the sign has *emotive* meaning.

Richards argued—wrongly, I have suggested—that emotive meaning is independent of descriptive meaning:

[1] Richards himself gives a more subtle exposition of his theory in *Coleridge on the Imagination* (1934) and *The Philosophy of Rhetoric* (1936).
[2] See Max Black on 'Emotive Meaning' in *The Philosophical Review*, March 1948, p. 122.

What matters is that the series of attitudes ... should have their own proper organisation; their own emotional interconnection, and this often has no dependence on the logical relations of such references as may be encountered in bringing the attitudes into being.[1]

Stevenson sees that the descriptive and emotive aspects of language are *interwoven*:

It is evident that a sign may have both kinds of meaning. That is to say, it may have at once a disposition to affect feelings or attitudes *and* a disposition to affect cognition. ... The growth of emotive and descriptive dispositions in language does not represent two isolated processes. There is a continual interplay.[2]

Stevenson goes on to make a point of the utmost importance. The two sorts of meaning often change, but they do not change together. For example, the descriptive meaning of a word may vary while the emotive meaning remains constant. This is one reason why the distinction between the two sorts of meaning matters so much. Stevenson illustrates this point with reference to the word 'democracy'.

He observes that this word 'democracy' has a pleasing emotive meaning to his fellow Americans because its descriptive meaning pleases them. In other words, they like 'government by the people' as practised under their own constitution, and, liking it, they like the word 'democracy' which in their language denotes that sort of government. But, Stevenson goes on to suggest:

Suppose, for example, that a group of people should come to disapprove of certain aspects of democracy, but continue to approve of other aspects of it. They might leave the descriptive meaning of 'democracy' unchanged, and gradually let it acquire, for their usage, a much less laudatory emotive meaning. On the other hand they might keep the strong laudatory [emotive] meaning unchanged, and let 'democracy' acquire a descriptive sense which made reference only to those aspects of democracy (in the other sense) which they favoured.[3]

Recent European history has illuminated Stevenson's point with

---

[1] *The Principles of Literary Criticism*, p. 268.
[2] C. L. Stevenson, *Ethics and Language* (New Haven, Conn., 1944), p. 71.
[3] *Ethics and Language*, p. 72.

interesting examples. In Germany the Nazis allowed the word 'demo-cracy' to retain its conventional descriptive meaning unaltered, but changed it to a pejorative word. In Eastern Europe the Communists have altered the conventional descriptive meaning of the word 'democracy' (so that it is used to refer to their own totalitarian style of government), but have allowed it to remain a laudatory word.

Of the two processes, the second is the more subtle and deceiving. It owes its success to what Stevenson calls the *inertia* of meaning.

> Suppose, [he suggests][1] that a term's laudatory emotive meaning has arisen *solely* because its descriptive meaning refers to something which people favour. And suppose that a given speaker succeeds in changing the descriptive meaning of the term in a way which his audience temporarily sanctions. One might expect that the emotive meaning will undergo a parallel change, automatically. But in fact it often will not. Through inertia it will survive a change in the descriptive meaning on which it originally depended.

That is why the Communists have been able to preserve the emotive meaning of 'democracy' while altering so radically the word's descriptive meaning.

§

The word 'freedom'—like its synonym 'liberty'—has a strong laudatory emotive meaning for English-speaking peoples, whether in political or more general use. But what of its descriptive meaning? That we have seen must vary with the context. In itself, the word 'freedom' cannot be said to have more than a *partial* descriptive mean-ing. For the word to be understood the listener must, as we have previously shown, understand what any particular freedom is freedom from or freedom for. What we have now seen is that while the descriptive meaning of 'freedom' thus varies, the emotive meaning tends, nevertheless, to be constant.

Some readers may suspect that this kind of analysis is dangerous; they may fancy it to have a Hobbesian tone, to recall some chapters of *Leviathan*. For Thomas Hobbes was also interested in the name of liberty; and he went on from a brisk analysis of the word to call it a 'specious name'[2] and to justify absolute government.

Is any analytic approach to the question of freedom open to a similar

---

[1] *Op. cit.*, p. 72.
[2] *Leviathan*, chap. xxv.

charge of illiberalism? We shall be reminded, perhaps, that subjects of
constitutional monarchs and citizens of the more fortunate republics
grow up in the love of freedom. Their freedom is their greatness and
their glory. But if I am right, the most *constant* thing in the meaning of
'freedom' is the tendency of the word to express and generate favourable feelings. Descriptively it may have any one of a vast range of
possible meanings. Apart from a particular context (and not always in its
context) there is no knowing precisely what 'freedom' may refer to.

Now, it may be said, these conclusions are cynical and destructive
of a free people's traditions and ideals; they play into the hands of
Hobbesians, Communists and Fascists.

I hope such suspicions are unjustified. They are nourished, perhaps,
by memories of Falstaff and notably of that shameful moment in
Henry IV[1] when Shakespeare's knight is called upon to fight for his
King. He pauses.

'What is honour?' he asks. 'A word. What is that word honour?
Air.'

And promptly on this reasoning, Falstaff acts dishonourably.

Falstaff was wrong. Honour is not a word. 'Honour' is a word. So
is 'freedom' and so is 'liberty'. But to say that 'freedom' and 'liberty'
are words, is certainly not to say (in the manner of Sir John) that
freedom is *only* a word, or even that freedom *is* a word.

[1] Part I, Act v, Scene i.

3

THEORIES

If freedom is not only a word, what is it? The literature of philosophy and politics abounds in answers to that question. And the answers are quite astonishingly various. I have already quoted those of Charles the First and Acton and Rousseau. We shall now consult some other oracles:

Duns Scotus: 'Liberty [is] a perfection of will.' (Copleston's *History of Philosophy*, II, pp. 532–3.)

Hobbes: 'Liberty, or freedom, signifieth, properly, the absence of opposition.' (*Leviathan*, XXI, i.)

Locke: '*Liberty* . . . is the power a man has to do or forbear doing any particular action.' (*Essay*, II, xxi, 15.)

Hume: 'By liberty we can only mean a power of acting according to the determination of the will.' (*Enquiry*, VIII, i, 73.)

Kant: Freedom is 'independence of anything other than the moral law alone.' (*Critique of Pure Reason*, Akademie edition, p. 93.)★

Leibniz: 'Freedom is spontaneity of the intelligence.' (*Werke*. Gerhardt's edition, VII, 108.)★

Hegel: 'Freedom is necessity transfigured.' (*Logik*, § 158.)★

Cohen: 'Freedom is the energy of the will.' (*Logik*, § 259.)★

Paulsen: 'Freedom for man is the government of spirit.' (*System der Ethik*, p. 442.)★

Bonnet: 'Freedom is the faculty by which the mind executes its will.' (*Essai*, XII, 149.)★

Heidegger: 'Freedom is "a participation in the revealment of what-is-as-such".' (*Existence and Being*, English edition, p. 334.)

Spinoza: 'A free man . . . is one who lives according to the dictate of reason alone.' (*Ethics*, Pt. IV, Prop. LXVII.)★

Schelling: 'Freedom is nothing but the absolute determination of the indeterminate through the bare natural laws of being.' (*Vom Ich*, p. 188.)★

★ Author's translation.

17

Engels: 'Freedom is control over ourselves and over external nature which is founded on knowledge of natural necessity.' (*Anti-Duhring*, Ch. xi.)

In this diverse list of answers to the question 'What is freedom?' there are two which are common to two distinct groups of philosophers. The first is the one which says that freedom is a faculty; the second is the one which says that freedom for human persons is government by reason. Let us look at these two groups in turn.

The notion that freedom is a faculty or power was, as we have seen, Locke's, and it was held by most of the philosophers who came under Locke's influence in France and Germany as well as in England. We have noted Hume's concept of freedom as power. Wolf,[1] Baumgarten[2] and Bilfinger[3] used the Latin word *facultas*; Bonnet, Voltaire[4] and Destutt de Tracy[5] were among French philosophers who wrote of freedom as *une faculté* or *le pouvoir*.

The doctrine of freedom as government by reason is a more elaborate one, and it is closely bound up with certain sorts of moral philosophy. Montesquieu is interesting in having held *both* the Lockean view that freedom is a faculty[6] and the view that freedom 'can consist only in the power of doing what we *ought* to will'.[7] This second view is held by Spinoza, Butler, Kant, Rousseau, Hegel, Bosanquet and Bradley; it is least adumbrated by Aristotle, and we have seen that Milton expressed it in his poetry. It has found widespread assent.

§

The notion that freedom is a faculty or power is, I believe, mistaken. In French the mistake may arise from the ambiguity of the word '*pourvoir*', which is both a transitive verb meaning 'to be able' and a masculine substantive meaning 'power'.

There may not seem much difference between being free to do a thing and being able to do a thing. Ignoring the difference, we could build up a simple syllogism thus:

[1] *Philosophia Practica Universalis*, i, § 12.
[2] *Metaphysica*, § 719, 529.
[3] *Dilucidationes Philosophicae*, § 301.
[4] *Le Philosophe Ignorant*, xiii, 70.
[5] *Eléments d'Idéologie*, iv, p. 108.
[6] *Esprit des Lois*, xii, 2.
[7] See Charles Morgan, *Liberties of the Mind* (London, 1951), pp. 57–80.

(a) Being free to is being able to;
(b) Being able to is having a power to;
Therefore
Being free to is having a power to;
Or, in short, freedom is a power.

The syllogism is formally valid, but it is vitiated by a premiss which is materially false. In the conventional use of our language, there *is* a difference between *being free to* and *being able to*, and it is not a difference we can afford to ignore. Likewise, in French, *'pouvoir'* the transitive verb is not the same as *'pouvoir'* the masculine substantive.

It is a tautology that a man cannot do a thing if he cannot do it. But a man does not say he is free to do a thing simply because he possesses the power or faculty to do it. When he says he can do something, he may mean he has a skill ('I can play Canasta'); or he may mean he has an opportunity ('I can send you some eggs'). He says he is free to do it only when he wants to refer to the absence of impediments in the way of doing it.

It is often said that freedom is 'empty' without power. The hunger marchers of the 1930s used to mock at their freedom to dine at the Ritz Hotel; because although there was no ban on the hunger marchers dining at the Ritz Hotel, no hunger marcher could afford to pay to dine there. It would be foolish to say you were free to play chess if you did not know how to play chess. But to say you can play chess is not to say you are free to play it.

The point can be made in another way. We indicate a man's freedom to do this or that by the word 'may' and not by the word 'can'.

Compare: 1. You may swim to the island,
2. You can swim to the island.

The first is a permissive declaration. The second is a statement about your abilities. For (1) to be valid it is only necessary that I should have the authority to say it, and say it. For (2) to be true it is necessary that you should be able to swim and swim well enough to reach the island.

Such are the considerations which tell against the Lockean doctrine that freedom is a faculty or power. Truly there is little point in 'being free to' unless we 'have the power to', but it certainly does not follow from this that the one is identical with the other.

§

The view that freedom for the human person is government by reason is generally advanced by philosophers who agree with Aristotle that there is something *mean* about the notion of freedom as the absence of constraint, which Aristotle epitomized as 'doing what one likes . . . each man living, as Euripides says, "For any end he chances to desire" '.[1]

It is not only the desire for something nobler which prompts this discontent with the vulgar notion of freedom. There is also a desire to seek out, in Kant's words, 'the positive in freedom'. But we cannot understand this concept of freedom unless we keep in focus the picture of man as these philosophers see him.

They see him as a rational creature—but not wholly rational. Besides his rational will, man is subject to the solicitations of impulses and desires which are not rational. Therefore, it is argued, the mere absence of constraint is not a sufficient condition of human freedom and hence not an adequate definition of the 'freedom' we speak of.

Such philosophers insist that in speaking of freedom with regard to human persons we are concerned with something which stands in marked contrast to what they often call (with Milton) *licence*, or the indulgence of non-rational desires and passions. Applying the word 'licence' to the indulgence of the non-rational element, they reserve the words 'freedom' and 'liberty' for the unfettered exercise of the rational will. For such theorists do not see man as a mere nexus of conflicting desires, but rather as a hierarchy of desires. Some desires are more important, more lasting, more essential to the nature of man than others. These are the desires sanctioned by human reason. Reason, so the familiar argument runs, is man's peculiar and essential characteristic. Thus in willing those ends which his reason sets before him, he is exhibiting his peculiar and essential nature. On the other hand, if his conduct is governed by the non-rational desires he shares with the beasts, he is not exhibiting his true nature, and is possibly betraying it. Kant said that rational desire (the good will) was most evident when it appeared in conflict with non-rational desire.

Thus, freedom is not just something that stands opposed to any one of many possible constraints and burdens. We might say that it is the absence of non-rational control of the human will. But rational theorists prefer positive terms. Freedom, they say, is something to be realized. The frustration of non-rational usurpation of the human will by the rational faculty is realized in self-discipline, in the maintenance of

---

[1] Aristotle, *Politics*, v, ix, §§ 15, 16.

reason's proper authority. And this is how certain philosophers have come to say that freedom is government—government by reason, conscience, *Geist, intellectus.*

This theory of rational freedom has produced a still more stringent variant which I shall call *enforceable rational freedom.*

We have seen that 'freedom' may mean freedom from many different things, including constraints imposed, so to speak, 'from within'. We are constrained by habit; we are constrained by inhibitions, and constrained by overwhelming desires. Theorists of rational freedom have concentrated on these inner constraints, at least on some of them. And concentrating on the inner constraints, these theorists have tended to overlook the constraints that originate in the outside world.

This has opened the way to the notion that external forces could be employed to *promote* freedom, that a man may be 'forced to be free'. Whereas, in ordinary usage, the word freedom stands opposed to constraint, this philosophical conception of freedom calls for the presence of constraint, first to assist the rational faculty in each individual to secure mastery over his non-rational faculties, and secondly, to clarify rational ends for people of limited intelligence.

This notion of *enforceable rational freedom* differs in a most crucial respect from the notion of *rational freedom* from which it derives. *Rational freedom* finds freedom in self-discipline. *Enforceable rational freedom* finds freedom in *discipline. Rational freedom* is thus individualistic, linked to a private ethic. *Enforceable rational freedom* is political— linked to a social ethic.

Enforceable rational freedom is the conception of freedom advanced by Spinoza, Rousseau (sometimes), Hegel and Bosanquet (and most English Hegelians). Aristotle, to some extent anticipated their conclusions, although he does not give such an account of freedom unequivocally. Newman, his Victorian translator, says:[1] 'Aristotle's view is that the governed are free when the government is exercised for their benefit.' Sir Ernest Barker, the author of a more recent translation,[2] writes:

> How would Aristotle himself have defined liberty? As Newman says, the passage (Book v, ix, §16 where Aristotle writes 'To live by the rule of the constitution ought not to be regarded as slavery

[1] *The Politics of Aristotle* (1887), vol. I, p. 246.
[2] *The Politics of Aristotle* (1948), p. 275, *n.* 3.

but rather as salvation') makes it probable that he would have defined it as obedience to rightly constituted law.

Different philosophers present different arguments for *enforceable rational freedom*. Most of them can be summarized in some such terms as these:

Rational freedom is realized in rational control. The study of history and of human behaviour teaches us what are the external conditions most favourable to, and those most detrimental to the exercise of rational control within the individual. Hence, in so far as favourable conditions can be established, indeed *enforced*, by those in authority in a community, such enforcement will promote the freedom of each individual.

There may be other philosophers who are drawn to the notion of compulsory freedom from sheer love of the paradox. Such an approach is well represented in the character of Leverkühn in Thomas Mann's novel *Dr. Faustus*:

> But freedom [Leverkühn says] is of course another word for subjectivity, and some fine day she does not hold out any longer, some time or other she despairs of being creative out of herself and seeks shelter and security in the objective. Freedom always inclines to dialectical reversals. She realizes herself in the sub-ordination to law, rule, coercion, system—but to fulfil herself therein does not mean that she therefore ceases to be freedom.

I have criticized the doctrine of freedom as a faculty on the ground that it rests on a mistake (the mistake of confusing 'being able to' with 'being free to'). My criticism of the doctrine that freedom is *rational* control, either self-imposed or imposed from without, involves more complicated argument. First I must confess to a doubt—a doubt whether the theory of *rational freedom* is really a theory about freedom. Then I shall go on to my criticism, which turns on the question of whether the theorists of *rational freedom* and *enforceable rational freedom* are defining the word 'freedom' and, if so, how their definitions are to be judged as definitions.

If the doctrine of *rational freedom* is not about freedom, what is it about? Let us consider. It is a doctrine which bifurcates the human person. It shows us man as made up of a rational self, which ought to be superior, and an animal or non-rational self, which ought to be subordinate, but which is always trying to usurp control. As sometimes expressed, the doctrine divides a man into a real self and unreal self. Bosanquet's version of *enforceable rational freedom*, for example, is based on such an analysis.

'Liberty', he writes,[1] 'must be a condition relevant to our continued struggle to assist the control of something in us, which we recognize as imperative on us or as our real self, but which we only obey in a very imperfect degree. Thus it is that we can speak, without a contradiction, of being forced to be free.'

One reason why such philosophers have a special theory about freedom is that they have a special theory about *the self*. Commonly the self is thought of as a whole 'mind-body' unit; these theorists distinguish a more rarefied self. And precisely because this (rational or real) self is not identical with the source of irrational desires, freedom for the (rational or real) self is not the same as freedom for the lower (animal or unreal) self from which irrational desires spring.

Accept this picture of the bifurcated man, and you do not need to make a case for *rational* freedom. If 'I am free' means 'My real self is free' and 'My real self' is the rational, reflective part of my being, no further revision of the concept of freedom is necessary. For it is clear that if your animal desires are not really *yours*, i.e. do not originate in your real self, you will not be free if their satisfaction is unimpeded. Since the special doctrine of the self thus entails that in such circumstances '*You* will not be free', it is otiose to add a special doctrine to show that in such circumstances 'You will not be *free*'.

[1] B. Bosanquet, *The Philosophical Theory of the State* (London, 1934), p. 117.

4

DEFINITIONS

We put the question 'What is freedom?' and we looked at the answers various philosophers have given to that question. So far I have called their answers 'theories' or 'concepts'; I have used such words because I did not want to prejudice the issues of the present chapter by calling them definitions'. Yet it would seem to be difficult to answer the question 'What is freedom?' without giving a definition of the word 'freedom'.

This in turn raises the odd-looking question: 'How do you define a definition?' John Holloway gives an acceptable definition of 'definition' in his book *Language and Intelligence*. He writes (p. 155): 'The word "definition" will be employed to refer to any process of making more precise the limits within which a word may be used.'

This process may take more than one form; there is thus more than one sort of definition. Two are of particular importance. The more familiar sort of definition takes the form of a report of the way in which, for example, an English word is used by English-speaking people in ordinary conversation. Most of the definitions given in dictionaries are of this sort, though the bigger dictionaries usually report also how the standard authors have severally employed that word. Definitions which report what words mean conventionally, what people commonly mean when they use them, may be called *lexicographical* definitions.

Not all definitions are reports. It often happens that a speaker or writer makes an announcement of the way in which *he* proposes to use a certain word, stipulates what the word is to stand for when *he* utters it. This may be called *stipulative* definition.

Stipulative definitions are often necessary, especially in science, because the conventional meanings of words are apt to be vague.

In poetry this vagueness of words often adds to the beauty and excitement of the verse, as William Empson has explained in his *Seven Types of Ambiguity*. Virginia Woolf once said:[1] 'Words hate

[1] *The Death of the Moth* (London, 1942), p. 131.

anything that stamps them with one meaning or confines them to one attitude, for it is their nature to change.'

Nevertheless there are times when it is necessary for the purposes of a particular discourse, to 'stamp one meaning' on a word. That is where the ambiguity of the conventional meaning hinders understanding. A speaker can usefully stipulate a new definition when the lexicographical definition is too indefinite or too ambiguous. The point is well expressed by Paul Valéry in *Regards sur le Monde Actuel* (p. 57):

> L'esprit, s'il s'attarde sur les termes qui se rencontrent le plus fréquemment en histoire et en politique, se perd assez rapidement dans ses tentatives de précision. Il veut qu'à chaque nom corresponde un objet sensible ou définissable—et un seule; et que chaque objet, dont il puisse ou doive reconnaître l'existence, porte un nom—et un seul. Mais l'usage, qui fait le dictionnaire, ne le fait *uniforme* ni *univoque*, car ces qualités ne peuvent résulter que de l'acte d'un seul esprit, ou (ce qui revient au même), de l'accord explicite de quelques-uns instituant et décrétant une *convention*.

Richard Robinson in his well-known book *Definition* (p. 66) writes:

> Learned and professional societies make stipulative definitions in order that intercourse between their members may not be rendered futile by such ambiguities. Thousands of arguments occur every day which are from a scientific point of view quite futile because the arguers either do not realize they are using a word in different senses, or, if they realize it, devote themselves to condemning all uses of the word but their own.

Robinson continues (p. 68):

> The greatest good to be obtained by stipulative definitions . . . is the improvement of concepts or the creation of new concepts, which is the key to one or two or three locks on the door of successful science. The notions summoned or held in mind by ordinary words, though rich in suggestions and poetry and emotions, and valuable for their suppleness and ease, have, owing to their vagueness and ambiguity, two defects that make them incapable of establishing science. Neither their applications nor their logical consequences are clear enough.

That is why it is so often necessary for careful writers, including scientists, to say 'By the word "x" I mean so-and-so'.

Notice, however, that such stipulative definitions differ in a most important respect from lexicographical definitions. Because lexicographical definitions *report* the way words are conventionally used they may be true or false, according to whether they report such usage accurately or inaccurately. Stipulative definitions, on the other hand, cannot be divided into the true and the false. They are arbitrary. You can stipulate that 'black' shall mean white, for example, by pointing to a patch of snow and saying 'Whenever I say "black" I mean this colour'. You can stipulate that a circle shall be square, by saying 'Whenever I say "circle" I mean an equilateral figure with four equal angles'. The possibilities of stipulative definitions are illustrated by the famous conversation between Alice and Humpty Dumpty in *Alice Through the Looking Glass*.

> 'When I use a word,' Humpty Dumpty said in rather a scornful tone, 'it means just what I choose it to mean—neither more nor less.'
>
> 'The question is,' said Alice, 'whether you can make words mean so many different things.'
>
> 'The question is,' said Humpty Dumpty, 'which is to be master—that's all.'

Although stipulative definitions cannot be divided into the true and the false, they may nevertheless be divided into the useful and the muddling. If stipulation is to be useful it needs to obey certain rules, notably the following:

1. All *other* definitions should be repudiated, since the proliferation of different meanings for the same word must increase ambiguity, and thus aggravate the confusion which stipulation was intended to end.

2. A new meaning should not be stipulated for a word if another word already has that meaning conventionally.

Rule 1 embodies a very simple principle. If a man announces that he uses a word to mean something he stipulates, and not in its conventional sense, his listeners will not misunderstand him provided they have heard *how* he uses that word and provided he *always* uses the word in that way. If he sometimes uses it as *he* has defined it and sometimes as it is defined in common use, nobody will ever be sure what he means. Readers of E. M. Forster's novel *A Passage to India* will remember a gentleman called Turton who holds *bridge parties*—'parties to bridge the gap between the races'—that is to say one who uses the expression 'bridge party' with a meaning he has stipulated and which is quite distinct from the lexicographical definition of the expression 'bridge party'. In the novel strangers are told how Mr Turton uses the expression, and those who know him know his definition. There is no misunderstanding because the stipulative definition in Mr Turton's conversation has *wholly* replaced the lexicographical definition. But if he had used the expression 'bridge party' on some occasions to mean 'a party to bridge the gap between the races', and at others to mean 'a party to play the game called bridge', there would be no knowing *which* he meant, and people who accepted Mr Turton's invitations could never be sure what sort of entertainment to expect.

Robinson gives the following rules for good stipulative definition:[1]

> (*a*) Stipulate as little as possible; (*b*) let us not stipulate until we have good reason to believe that the phrase which already covers our designatum is too cumbrous for our purposes; (*c*) let us not stipulate until we have good reason to believe that there is no name for the thing we wish to name; (*d*) let us not stipulate different symbols to mean the same thing; (*e*) let us not stipulate one symbol for two different things.

§

We have put the question 'What is freedom?' to several philosophers; and we have noticed some of their answers. *Prima facie* to answer the question 'What is freedom?' is to give a definition of 'freedom'. When Locke and his successors said 'freedom is a faculty', they were defining 'freedom' as 'a faculty'; surely, again, when the other theorists said 'freedom is government by reason' they too were defining 'freedom'? And what are such statements as 'Freedom is necessity transfigured' (Hegel), 'Freedom is the energy of the will' (Cohen), 'Freedom is the determination of the indeterminable through the bare natural laws of being' (Schelling), and 'Freedom is participation in what-is-assuch' (Heidegger)—what are all these if they are not also definitions of the word 'freedom'?

If they *are* definitions, three further questions will immediately arise.
1. Are they lexicographical or stipulative definitions?
2. If they are lexicographical definitions, do they report accurately? (Are they true or false?)
3. If they are stipulative definitions, are they useful? (Do they satisfy the rules of good stipulative definition?)

[1] R. Robinson, *Definition* (Oxford, 1950), p. 80.

The model of lexicographical definition is usually provided by a dictionary. *The Concise Oxford Dictionary*, in a two-column entry on the word 'free', defines 'free' as among other things:

> (1) Not in bondage to another . . . (2) loose, unrestricted, at liberty, not confined, released from ties or duties, unimpeded, unfettered in action, permitted to be independent . . .

Hobbes wishes to give a lexicographical definition of the words when he wrote:[1]

> 'Liberty', or 'freedom', signifieth, properly, the absence of opposition—by opposition I mean external impediments of motion; and may be applied no less to irrational and inanimate creatures than to rational.

The first two chapters of this essay may be read as a kind of preface to a definition of the words 'free', 'freedom', 'liberty'. Words cannot always be defined briefly. Some people write a whole book in defining a word. Plato's *Republic* might be read as such a book-length definition of 'justice'—but that is perhaps an example of stipulative definition. The first chapters of this essay are intended to contribute to a lexicographical definition. And because they are intended to give a lexicographical definition—a report on the way the word 'free' is used by English-speaking people generally—that definition may be true or false.

The same may be said of Hobbes's definition. That is also a lexicographical definition of the word 'freedom'. I have suggested it is not strictly a true one. Hobbes says the word 'freedom' stands for *less* than what it does conventionally stand for. He says, rightly as far as he goes, that 'freedom' is 'absence of opposition'. But we have seen that 'freedom' means also 'absence of constraints and burdens'. And when Hobbes goes on to define 'opposition' as 'external impediments of motion' he confines the meaning of the word 'freedom' still more narrowly. In fact, as we have seen, the word 'freedom' may equally represent the absence of *internal, self-imposed* or *self-generated* constraints.

What of the definition of freedom as a faculty? This, too, is a *lexicographical* definition. It was intended to be an account of what people commonly mean when they talk about their freedom. In criticizing this doctrine, I argued that people do *not* mean they have a

---

[1] *Leviathan*, chap. xxi.

faculty when they say they are free; and thus that there was a reporting error in the *faculty* definition of the word. It was meant to be a lexicographical definition, but it was not a true one.

The theorist who defined 'freedom' as 'government by reason' could hardly be said to be giving a lexicographical definition of 'freedom'. For this is manifestly *not* what English-speaking people commonly mean when they use the word 'freedom'.

It may be suggested that it is a lexicographical definition in a more limited sense, namely a definition of 'freedom' as that word is always used in philosophical as distinct from general conversation. This argument could certainly find some backing from publications which call themselves Dictionaries of Philosophy. We may note, for example, in America, a *Dictionary of Philosophy*, edited by Dagobert D. Runes, published in 1944, and in France a *Vocabulaire de la Philosophie*, edited by André Lalande, in 1951. The American dictionary gives only one, a brief Kantian definition of 'freedom' as 'the autonomy or self-determination of rational beings'; the French *vocabulaire* gives several definitions of '*liberté*' including a rational definition which is described as the 'philosophical' sense of the word.

We have already noticed in Rousseau a reference to 'the philosophical sense' of the word 'freedom', and this, apparently, is what these Dictionaries of Philosophy have wished to specify. Their enterprise is surely an unfortunate one. For nothing is more immediately evident to the readers of philosophical books than the fact that all philosophers do *not* use the word 'freedom' in one and the same way. I have discussed two groups of philosophers who use the word in two particular ways, and outside those groups there are many more philosophers who use the word 'freedom' in ways which differ from both. There may be one or two technical terms in philosophy which all philosophers use in the same way—'analytic', 'synthetic', 'metaphysical', are possible examples; but it would be hard to think of many more. Even words like 'sense-data', 'realism' and 'idealism' are differently used by different philosophers. Indeed, philosophy has nothing like the technical vocabulary that, for example, chemistry and music have. That is why Dictionaries of Philosophy are so unsatisfactory. They suggest that there *are* fixed technical terms in philosophy corresponding to those of chemistry and music, when in fact there are not.

Since there is no one way in which philosophers use the word 'freedom', there can be no limited or 'technical' lexicographical definition of the word, constituting a report of the way in which philosophers always use it in their work. The so-called 'philosophical' definitions of 'freedom' report only how *some* (nothing like a majority of) philosophers use the word.

From this it follows that to define 'freedom' as 'government by reason' is to offer neither a general nor a limited or 'technical' lexicographical definition of the word. Is it not, rather, to give a *stipulative* definition? Such, indeed, is what such a pronouncement as 'freedom is government by reason' looks like. And why should not philosophers stipulate? Anyone can stipulate if he pleases. We did, however, notice some rules which need to be obeyed if a stipulative definition is to be useful.

How far do the utterances of the *rational* theorists satisfy those rules? Rule 1 demanded that a man who stipulates a new definition for a particular word should repudiate all other definitions. Do the theorists of rational freedom do this? If they speak of the 'freedom' of Ireland, do they mean that the Irish are now 'governed by reason'? If Kantians sit in divorce courts and grant 'freedom' to petitioners, do they grant 'independence of anything other than the moral law alone'? If Hegelians are mayors and grant the 'freedom' of their cities, do they bestow 'necessity transfigured'? If they do, its transfiguration is remarkable indeed.

In fact, of course, such philosophers do *not* propose to annul all previous meanings of the word 'free' as the rules ordain. Evidently, what they wish to do is to use the word as stipulatively defined only in *some* of the cases in which they use it. We have seen that such equivocation can only lead to more and more confusion. If a man uses a word in one sense at one time and in a profoundly different sense at another, his hearers will never be sure what he means when he uses it.

The second rule for good stipulation provided that no new word should be stipulated if an existing word, lexicographically defined, had precisely that meaning. I have already suggested that the theorists of *rational freedom* did not need to stipulate a new definition of freedom because their doctrine that only the rational element in the human person can be free followed from the metaphysical doctrine held by most of them, according to which only the rational element in the human person is real. Such theorists had therefore no need to stipulate a new definition of the word 'free'. Theorists of *enforceable rational freedom*, however, were seen to be in a different situation. For their belief that freedom may and should be enforced by external authority cannot be deduced from the doctrine that only the rational element in the human person is real. The doctrine of *enforceable rational freedom* involves a complete repudation of the conventional antithesis between 'freedom' and 'enforcement'; and this can only be done by a complete repudiation of the lexicographical definition of the word 'free' and the stipulation of another definition to take its place. It can nevertheless be seen that theorists of *enforceable rational freedom* are redefining 'freedom' to serve the purpose that an existing word already serves. 'Discipline' stands in ordinary English usage for what the theorists of *enforceable rational freedom* propose that the word 'freedom' shall represent. But why should such theorists delete 'discipline' and insert 'freedom'? The answer is a simple one. It is because 'freedom' is always a laudatory word and 'discipline', except, perhaps, for schoolmasters, officers, and policemen, has only a limited appeal.

Some of the philosophers I have criticized have actually offered (or suggested that the English language contains) *two* definitions of the word 'freedom'. Here I do not refer to those who have distinguished one genuine (their own) definition and another spurious (the vulgar) definition, but to those who have acknowledged besides their first (philosophical) definition a second genuine (if perhaps inferior) one. Martin Buber, for example, in his book *Between Man and Man* distinguishes a higher and a lower freedom. H. J. Paton in *The Categorical Imperative* (p. 267) claims that even Kant recognized two senses of the word 'freedom'.

We have seen the danger of using one word with two meanings. To avoid confusion a writer who upheld a double definition would need to put some sign against the word 'freedom' in either or both his two senses such as 'freedom (v)' and 'freedom (ph)' to distinguish the vulgar definition from the philosophical definition. The historian or critic might need further marks. The 'freedom (ph)' of Schelling for instance, will need to be distinguished from the 'freedom (ph)' of Heidegger by some such marks as 'freedom (ph. Sch.)' and 'freedom (ph. Heid.)'.

A bad way out of the difficulty has been suggested by Sir Herbert Read. He bases this recommendation on the fact that there are two words in the English language, 'freedom' and 'liberty', and he goes on to say that the word 'freedom' stands for what Buber calls 'higher freedom' and the word 'liberty' for what Buber calls 'lower freedom'. In the journal *Question* (II, 2, p. 198) Sir Herbert writes:

In English . . . we have two words: 'liberty' and 'freedom'. It is an advantage which most languages do not possess. Personally I think there is a distinction between these words and that it is an important one. I would say that 'liberty' indicates a state of body and 'freedom' a state of mind.

Elsewhere (in *Anarchism, Marxism and Existentialism*, p. 21), Read complains of too *glib* use of the word 'freedom'.

The 'freedom' of the press, the 'freedom' of association, the 'freedom' of trade— all such uses of the word seem to me wrong, for freedom is an abstract concept, a philosophical word.

Read presumably holds that the correct word in such contexts is not 'freedom' but 'liberty'. He then goes on to make the interesting point that while the French language contains the word '*liberté*', it has no second word for 'freedom', and while the German language contains the word '*Freiheit*' it has no further word for 'liberty'. We are thus prompted to believe that the French can understand the common notion of liberty but not the philosophical notion of freedom, while the Germans can understand the philosophical notion of freedom, but not the common notion of liberty. It is a plausible point, and very flattering to English and American readers, but it will not do.

There *are* differences between the words 'freedom' and 'liberty', but they are not the differences Read suggests. He writes as if he were reporting facts about the use of the English language. It is not a fact about that language that 'freedom' stands for what Buber calls 'higher freedom' and that 'liberty' stands for what Buber calls 'lower freedom'. In English usage the words 'freedom' and 'liberty' are virtually interchangeable. The word 'liberty' tends to be used in legal and political contexts, 'freedom' in philosophical and more general ones. It would be hard to write an English sentence containing the word 'liberty' in which the word 'freedom' could not take its place without alteration of meaning. A small difference is that the noun 'freedom' co-exists with an adjective 'free', while the noun 'liberty' has no adjective (although '*liberté*' in French, of course, has '*libre*'). Apart from this, everything I have hitherto said about 'freedom' applies equally to 'liberty'. The choice of one word or the other is usually a matter of literary style.

5

PERSUASION

We return to emotive meaning. The *rational* and *enforceable rational* definitions of the word 'freedom' have failed to satisfy the rules of good stipulation. This does not mean they are altogether futile. They are useless in the sense that they fail to increase clarity. But it may be they have another use. They may serve to *exploit* ambiguity in order to achieve a certain effect. They may be what Stevenson calls 'persuasive definitions'.

Persuasive definitions, Stevenson explains,[1] aim at altering the descriptive meaning of a term without altering its emotive meaning so that they may direct the hearer's favourable feelings towards a new object.

We have seen that the word 'freedom' kindles favourable feelings, that it kindles them because people generally feel well disposed towards what the word ordinarily stands for—the absence of bondage, opposition, constraints, impediments, burdens. The theorists of *rational freedom* have assured people that they are right to have these feelings towards the word 'freedom' but they have gone on to tell them that the word 'freedom' does not mean what they think it means—the absence of bondage, opposition, constraints, impediments, burdens; the word 'freedom', they say, means x or y or z, and 'x' or 'y' or 'z' is each philosopher's *persuasive definition*.

Such a fate is not peculiar to the word 'free'. Most *hurrah* words which do not correspond to what Valéry calls *un objet sensible*, tend to be persuasively defined. 'Art' is persuasively defined in Tolstoi's *What is Art*, 'poetry' in A. E. Housman's *Name and Nature Poetry*, 'culture' in T. S. Eliot's *Notes towards the Definition of Culture*.[2]

Nor is persuasive definition a practice peculiar to scholars. Plain men say such things as:

'Religion is anything a man believes in deeply.'
'The true liberal is a Tory.'

[1] *Ethics and Language*, p. 206.
[2] Robinson, *op. cit.*, pp. 167–9.

'True temperance is a bottle of claret with each meal and three double whiskies after dinner.'[1]

The word 'true' is often the mark of a persuasive definition. Ironically so; for the whole point about such definitions is that they are *neither* true *nor* false. Only lexicographical definitions are true or false. Persuasive definitions, like all other stipulative definitions, are arbitrary.

What is the difference between persuasive definition and sound stipulative definition? A man who stipulates soundly says, 'This is how *I* use the word "x" '. A man who gives a persuasive definition is trying to make *you* believe that the way *he* uses the word 'x' is the *correct* way.

Persuasive definition is the foundation of the alarming language 'Newspeak' invented by George Orwell in his prophetic novel *1984*. His scene is a Communist Utopia where standard English has been replaced by a language suited to the ideological needs of the new State. In Newspeak, 'War is peace', 'Freedom is slavery', 'Ignorance is strength'. The organs of the State are a Ministry of Truth, which issues lying propaganda; a Ministry of Peace, which concerns itself with war, a Ministry of Love, which supervises punishment and the police, and a Ministry of Plenty, which distributes the meagre rations. Orwell explains Newspeak thus:

> Its vocabulary was so constructed as to give exact and often very subtle expression to every meaning that a Party member could properly wish to express, while excluding all other meanings and also the possibility of arriving at them by indirect methods. This was done . . . chiefly by eliminating undesirable words and by stripping such words as remained of unorthodox meanings, and so far as possible of all secondary meanings whatever.[2]

Orwell puts Newspeak in the future. But the practice of persuasive definition, on which it is based, is as old as the art of rhetoric.

§

If either or both the *rational* and *enforceable rational* theories of freedom constitute persuasive definitions, the question arises as to whether they have been successful or unsuccessful? Have they persuaded?

The evidence of history and sociology and social psychology shows that they have enjoyed a considerable success. How has this come about?

[1] This example comes from Aldous Huxley. There is an excellent discussion of persuasive definition in *Eyeless in Gaza* (*The Diary of Anthony Beavis*).

[2] *1984* (first London edition, 1949), p. 299.

1. The success of the *rational* definition seems largely due to the fact that very many people besides Aristotle, and not only philosophers, have thought that freedom understood as the absence of constraint is a *mean* conception. Because 'freedom' is a laudatory word, people will readily agree that 'freedom is good', and since 'good' is an ethical word, they can be persuaded that being free is having an ethical quality; and thus that only good actions are free actions, and only good men free men.

2. The success of the *enforceable rational* definition is more perplexing. How can intelligent people be persuaded to accept as the true definition of the word, one which directly contradicts its lexicographical definition?

The explanation is perhaps to be found in the dissatisfaction some people—again perhaps not a few—have felt in being unconstrained, in 'freedom' in the sense of freedom from external compulsion to act and even to live in a specific way.

André Gide, in his preface to *Vol de Nuit* by Antoine de St Exupéry, wrote:

> I am particularly grateful to St. Exupéry for throwing light on this paradoxical truth, for me considerably important psychologically: that a man's happiness lies not in freedom, but in the acceptance of a duty.

Here Gide is using the word 'freedom' as lexicographically defined and narrowed down by the context to mean 'freedom from social institutions (such as an army, state or church)'. St Exupéry was an aviator; he was happy flying under orders, when he had a duty to perform. He was not happy when he was left to his own devices. Gide made the same confession about himself; and it is a confession which incidentally helps the reader to understand why Gide was for so long opposed to liberalism. Having been rich enough and lucky enough to get his own way for most of his life, he was tempted in the melancholy times by which all selfish hedonists are afflicted, to believe that he preferred to be constrained.

Nicholas Berdyaev has written:[1]

> Man easily forgoes his liberty[2] for the sake of peace and happiness; he bears the heavy burden of it with difficulty and is only too

---

[1] *Freedom and the Spirit* (London, 1935), p. 127.

[2] The context makes it clear that Berdyaev, too, means 'liberty from the constraints of social institutions'.

ready to shift it on to stronger shoulders. . . . We see examples of this abdication of freedom by man and this preference for compulsion as well in the old theocratic theories as in the new ideas of socialism.

Berdyaev's view is reinforced by Erich Fromm in *The Fear of Freedom* which reports, as a sociological fact, that many people being unhappy when they are unconstrained, prefer compulsion. When the Roman Catholic Bishop of Brentwood (the Rt Rev. George A. Beck) some years ago attacked the liberal doctrine of the Rights of Man as containing 'insidiously corrosive influences', he added: 'Men are sick of running around in circles. They want to be told what to do.'[1]

It is not difficult to see how those people who are happiest when they are constrained could be persuaded that 'freedom' (still a laudatory word) does not *really* mean the absence of such welcome constraint, but its presence; that *true* freedom consists in being made to do what is right.

This circumstance, I believe, goes a long way towards explaining the success of *enforceable rational freedom* as a persuasive definition.

§

What I have hitherto written in this chapter may rest on a mistake— at least so far as *rational freedom* (as distinct from *enforceable rational freedom*) is concerned. Perhaps the philosophers concerned were not giving *definitions* in reply to our question 'What is freedom?' And if they were not giving definitions, they cannot be said to have been giving persuasive definitions.

I have suggested that these philosophers *need* not (for the most part) give a new definition of the word 'freedom' in view of the metaphysical theory which most of them hold. We must therefore consider carefully the argument that they are *not* giving a definition. It is likely to run as follows:

Not all sentences of the form 'freedom is x' are definitions of the word 'freedom'. The sentence 'freedom is dangerous' is not, of course, a definition of 'freedom'. Only such sentences of the form 'freedom is x' which specify or limit the use of the word 'freedom' are definitions of 'freedom'.

The theorists of *rational freedom* (the argument may continue) are

---

[1] *Manchester Guardian*, 21 April 1951.

not specifying or limiting the use of the word 'freedom'. What they are saying is something on the lines of the Christian precept: 'The service of God is perfect freedom.' This precept is not a definition of 'freedom'; it simply proclaims that this *sort* of freedom is the best of all freedoms. Likewise, the sentence 'freedom is government by reason' should be taken to mean 'the *best* freedom is government by reason' or 'the *most important* freedom for the human person is freedom from the domination of the non-rational part of his own nature'. Far from being a definition of 'freedom', this is a statement about the sort of freedom which is most meritorious. It is a *value judgment*.

How far is this argument acceptable?

Certainly, I think, the Christian precept that 'the service of God is perfect freedom' *is* a value judgment and not a definition of the word 'freedom'. C. S. Peirce for example, has interpreted the precept as saying that freedom from worldly things which accompanies the acceptance of service to God is conspicuously better than freedom from any other constraint or burden.

But is this to the point? None of the theorists of *rational* freedom has spoken of '*perfect* freedom'; they have spoken of 'freedom', and those who have spoken of '*true* freedom' have surely used the word 'true' as opposed to 'false', and not as opposed to 'inferior'?

Nor do I think all the philosophers concerned would accept this rendering of their doctrine, or this defence of their position. In their writings the word 'freedom' stands for something positive. If it does not do so in common usage, so much the worse, as some of them have said, for common usage.

Admittedly, to call the sentence 'freedom is government by reason' a value judgment, is not, in some people's view, to preclude that sentence from saying something about reality. For many of the philosophers concerned would hold that values 'inhere in reality'. Yet to say that the sentence 'freedom is government by reason' is only a value judgment and to deny that the sentence constitutes a definition of 'freedom' might well seem to the philosophers concerned to be disposing too cheaply of their wisdom.

§

A second argument may be urged against me, to run as follows:

'The *freedom* with which some, at least, of the theorists of *rational freedom* are concerned is the freedom of the will, that is, the principle which stands opposed to determinism. In saying that "freedom" means rational freedom they are saying that human conduct is determined (according to natural necessity) unless it originates in the rational self, which alone enjoys freedom from such necessity.

'Plainly, philosophers who are thinking freedom as opposed to determinism will not be concerned with external constraint, because if "freedom" is understood *only* as that which stands opposed to determinism it is not something which stands opposed to external constraints. When such philosophers say that external constraints are irrelevant, and that what is essential for human freedom is that the rational and not the irrational element should be in control, they are thinking of free will; they are saying, in effect, "the freedom *of the will* consists in government by reason".'

This defence may be used on behalf of both *rational freedom* and *enforceable rational freedom*. But how successfully?

I should not deny that *some* philosophers of *rational freedom*, and notably Kant, were preoccupied, when they wrote of freedom, with the freedom of the will. But I find no authority for thinking that whenever Kant spoke of freedom, which he once expressed as 'independence of anything other than the moral law alone',[1] he *always* meant the freedom of the will. Nor can I discover any other prominent champion of *rational freedom* (or *enforceable rational freedom*) of whom one could say that he used the word 'freedom' invariably to mean 'freedom of the will'. Spinoza believed in 'rational freedom' but denied the possibility of the freedom of the will; *he* cannot therefore have meant by the 'freedom' he recognized 'freedom of the will'. But supposing I concede the point. Then another dilemma will appear. There are, as we shall presently consider, certain objections to the phrase 'the freedom of the will'. In more than one way it is a misleading expression of the principle which stands opposed to determinism; that principle can, I shall suggest, be better expressed without using the word 'freedom' or the word 'will'. So what are we to say to a procedure which would *confine* the word 'freedom' to expressing the 'freedom of the will', and as a result of thus confining its meaning, makes it possible to use it only where there is no need to use it, and prevents its significant use in those cases where we are most accustomed to using it?

§

Coleridge, no enemy of metaphysics, once wrote in his notebook:

[1] *Critique of Practical Reason* (Akademie edition, p. 93).

'Generally indeed I complain of the German Philosophers (as we are apt to complain of our dearest Friends)—of the post-Kantians at least, for the precipitation with which they pass to their own determination of what the *thing* is, without having first enquired what the *word* means when it is used appropriately.'[1]

Where the word 'freedom' is concerned, the fault is by no means confined to 'post-Kantians' or to the three schools of thought I have so far considered. Even Coleridge himself defined 'freedom' in a way which differs from the lexicographical definition.[2]

Writers continue to issue new definitions of 'freedom' seasonally. Patrick Gordon Walker in his book *Restatement of Liberty* writes: 'liberty is an arduous pursuit of a goal that is never reached. It resides within men as well as without them and . . . can be enjoyed only by those who earn it and make their society a fit abode for freedom.' Michael Polanyi in his book *The Logic of Liberty* asserts that to be 'free' is to be 'fully dedicated to a distinctive set of beliefs'.

One paradoxical redefinition of the word 'freedom' which has received the widest currency is that of Marxist philosophy. 'Freedom', Marx and his followers say, 'is the recognition of necessity.' This is a definition which derives from Hegel, and which is reached by an exercise of dialectical logic. It is thus a mediate and not an immediate definition. 'Freedom' is first defined as the antithesis of necessity. Then by a familiar process of dialectical method, the antitheses are resolved and freedom is made to embrace necessity.

Grant the antithesis of freedom and necessity (which Hobbes and Hume and A. J. Ayer do not, but which the *Oxford English Dictionary* does[3]) and grant the validity of Hegel's logic, then it is reasonable to accept the Marxist conclusion that 'freedom is the recognition of necessity', although Hegel's own definition 'freedom *is* necessity transfigured' expresses the dialectical conclusion more felicitously.

It is, however, most unlikely that the widespread acceptance of the Marxist definition of 'freedom' follows from any such strenuous mental exercise. People who know nothing of dialectical logic think

[1] MS quoted in *Inquiring Spirit* (1951) by Kathleen Coburn.

[2] Freedom 'consists not merely in the enjoyment of equal laws, as human wisdom can plan and adopt, but in such security of the enjoyment of equal laws, as human wisdom can plan and adopt, and human courage and patriotism realise'. (MS quoted by Miss Coburn, *op. cit.*, p. 318.)

[3] I shall consider this antithesis in my chapters on the problem of the freedom of the will.

Marx is right. They think so, perhaps, for a reason suggested by Ayer in an article he wrote for *Polemic* 5 (p. 40):

> One of the reasons why people are inclined to define freedom as the consciousness of necessity is that they think that if one is conscious of necessity one may somehow be able to master it. But this is a fallacy. It is like someone's saying that he wishes he could see into the future, because if he did he would know what calamities lay in wait for him and so would be able to avoid them. But if he avoids the calamities, they don't lie in the future and it is not true that he foresees them. And similarly if I am able to master necessity, in the sense of altering the operation of necessary law, then the law in question is not necessary. And if the law is not necessary, then neither my freedom nor anything else can consist in my knowing that it is.

Ayer's wording suggests a view which differs slightly from my own. The fallacy he discusses leads people, he says, '*to define* freedom as the consciousness of necessity'. I have said it leads people to *accept* such a definition. The Hegelian-Marxian reconciliation of freedom and necessity does not rest on the fallacy Ayer exposes, although there are certainly other fallacies in the system of dialectical logic through which the definition was originally reached. Nevertheless, the fallacy Ayer mentions does, I believe, occur in the reasoning of many less sophisticated believers in the Marxist doctrine; and it is *because* such innocents have thus deceived themselves that the Marxist definition of 'freedom' as 'the recognition of necessity' has successfully persuaded them.

The Marxist definition may also owe some of its persuasive success to the factors already mentioned as favouring the success of *enforceable rational freedom*. In the field of practical politics the 'freedom' which the Marxist offers is also a 'compulsory' freedom. 'Recognition of necessity' for the citizens of Marxist republics and the members of Marxist parties is, in fact, 'obedience to orders'.

Just because this freedom which is defined in theory as necessity is in practice compulsion, such 'freedom' will attract the sort of people for whom the condition of being unconstrained by some external authority is not an agreeable condition; it will attract those who like to be coerced.

§

The *Existentialist* theory of freedom affords a striking contrast to

Marxist freedom and to *enforceable rational freedom*. Like many votaries of those philosophies, the Existentialists are uneasy in the absence of constraint or compulsion, but the Existentialists have no desire to use the word 'freedom' to mean anything different from what it generally means—the absence of constraint, compulsion, impediments, burdens. They do not wish to alter the descriptive meaning of the word 'freedom'. They wish to alter its emotive meaning. The Existentialists suggest that the word 'freedom' should be changed from a *hurrah*-word to what might be called a *dread*-word. They believe the appropriate attitude to the word 'freedom' should not be one of pleasure or approval but terrified apprehension.

Heidegger, it is true, gives a stipulative definition of 'freedom' as 'participation in the revealment of what-is-as-such', but in this he is not a representative Existentialist. Sartre is the Existentialist philosopher most interested in freedom, and he nowhere expresses any wish to define the word anew. He works on the assumption that people know what 'freedom' stands for. His concern is to alter their feelings towards what it stands for; and to confess his own ' . . . my fear is free and is a manifestation of my freedom; I put all my freedom into my fear . . .'

Dr Marjorie Grene's exposition of Existentialism has the apt title *Dreadful Freedom*. She writes, explaining the Existentialist attitude of freedom, thus:[1]

> Freedom reveals itself . . . when we screw up our courage to see it without pretence, in the dizzying collapse of external sanctions and universal law, in the appalling consciousness that I, and I alone, have absurdly and without reason, brought order out of chaos; that I alone, crudely and stupidly, without cosmic reason or rational ground, have made a world out of nothing: and with that awareness, my world itself totters on the brink of the nothingness from which it came.

To a man who is unhappy when he is not under some compelling superior but who still thinks that freedom ought to be agreeable, the Existentialist does not say (with other philosophers we have considered): 'That is because you are not *really* free when you are unconstrained; you are free when you are rightly governed'; on the contrary, the Existentialist says: 'You ought not to expect freedom to be agreeable.'

Gide expressed the Existentialist attitude when he wrote in his

[1] *Dreadful Freedom* (Chicago, 1948), p. 52.

Journal for 15 November 1928: 'I can assure you that the feeling of *freedom* can plunge the soul into a sort of anguish.' Gide was not, of course, an Existentialist, but the Existentialist message is addressed to those who feel, as he felt, 'a sort of anguish'. It has even given them a name for their feeling: '*Angst.*'

It is not surprising that the most important Existentialists should prove to be artists rather than pure philosophers: Kierkegaard, Sartre, Camus, Marcel, are all primarily men of letters. We have seen that Existentialism aims at directing *feelings*, as much as, if not more than, thoughts. In the matter of freedom, their attention is concentrated on the emotive, not on the descriptive meaning of the word. Emotive meanings are not altered by reasoning and logic so much as by experience and imagination.

§

Yet one must not exaggerate. However great the number of people who are uneasy when they are unconstrained, there remain many more, especially in the British Isles and America, in Switzerland and Holland and Israel and Scandinavia, in Australasia and—despite the Monarchists and Communists and Existentialists—in Italy and France, who understand freedom as the absence of constraint and like it; love it, indeed, and cherish it to the point of death.

W. H. Auden has said:[1] 'Liberty is not a value, but the ground of value.' Herbert Read, intending to correct him, has insisted:[2] 'freedom *is* a value, and indeed the value of all values'. Berdyaev has said:[3] 'Freedom is . . . the inner dynamic of the spirit, the irrational mystery of being, of life and of destiny.' John Lewis has gone even further: 'Freedom is the name for the totality of human goods, satisfactions and aspirations, material and spiritual.'[4]

We should not read such sentences as these as definitions of freedom, but rather as lines of praise to freedom by mean who love freedom. Martin Buber once said 'I love freedom, but I do not believe in it'. We may wonder how this paradoxical utterance is to be interpreted, but there must certainly be many who love freedom without being able to give an analysis of what they mean by it.

[1] In his Introduction to *The American Scene* by Henry James (New York, 1950).
[2] *Existentialism, Anarchism and Marxism* (London, 1949), p. 23.
[3] *Freedom and the Spirit*, p. 121.
[4] *Question*, vol. II, no. 2, p. 141. The utterance comes curiously from John Lewis, who is a Marxist.

I have written sceptically of Acton's project of writing the history of mankind as the history of its struggle towards freedom. Yet I believe it would be possible to write a history of political philosophy as a history of thought about freedoms and constraints. Such a project has, in a measure, been outlined. I have before me the syllabus of a course of lectures prepared by Professor Richard Peters for the University of London. In his introductory note, Professor Peters suggests that the terminology of freedom and constraint can be employed in discussing 'most of the persistent problems discussed by social philosophers', and he shows how such questions 'relate closely to most of our major social and political problems today, which are concerned with re-conciling the claims of individuals to express themselves in various spheres with those of others who may suffer as the result of such expression'.

This is not to suggest that political philosophy is a narrow subject. On the contrary, it indicates that the problems of freedom and constraint are exceedingly wide.

Part 2

THE AMBIGUITY OF LIBERALISM

I

ENGLISH LIBERALISM

A liberal, I suppose one could say, is a person who believes in liberty, as a nudist is a person who believes in nudity. But 'nudity' stands for one thing whereas 'liberty' (or 'freedom') stands, as we have seen, for different things in different contexts. It follows that if a 'liberal' is 'a person who believes in liberty', the meaning of 'liberal' must vary as the meaning of 'liberty' varies. Liberalism as understood in England in 1910 differs radically from liberalism as understood in Germany in 1848, and both differ in turn from liberalism as understood in the United States of America in 1967. Liberals have sometimes been painfully surprised to find how little they have had in common with foreign gentlemen to whom they have been introduced as fellow liberals. They would have been less surprised if they had remembered the lesson of the first great English liberal philosopher, Locke: 'It is impossible to speak clearly and distinctly of our knowledge, which all consists in propositions, without considering first the nature, use and signification of language.'[1] For if they had considered first the nature, use and signification of the word 'liberty', they would have seen that to proclaim belief in liberty is to proclaim no more than the prolegomenon to a political opinion.

To write about liberalism in more than a domestic context one must write about *liberalisms*. Historians who have failed to acknowledge this have had inevitably to fall back, often without realizing what they were doing, on stipulative definition. The universal liberalism they have analysed is 'liberalism' as defined by them, not 'liberalism' as variously understood by other people. In 1936 Harold J. Laski published a book entitled *The Rise of European Liberalism*; in 1946, John H. Hallowell published one called *The Decline of Liberalism*. The rising liberalism Laski describes is quite unlike the declining liberalism described by his successor. 'Liberalism' for Laski means nothing other than the political manifestation of bourgeois capitalism; to Hallowell 'liberalism' is a political doctrine resting on a belief in the supreme moral worth of the

[1] *Essay Concerning Human Understanding*, II, xxxiii, 19.

individual. Guido de Ruggiero in his *History of European Liberalism* discerns the variety of political doctrines which have been known as 'liberalism'; and the merit of his book is precisely that he does discern it. Before we follow his example and look at some of these different varieties of liberalism, I propose to consider the meaning of the word 'liberal' in the English usage of the British Isles (the American usage I shall examine later). The word is much newer to these islands than the political doctrine it stands for. Historians often say that Locke was a liberal and the Glorious Revolution a triumph for liberalism, yet no one spoke of 'liberals' in 1688 and 1689. The word was first heard in England in the early nineteenth century, when liberals were thus dubbed by their political opponents. They were called, in fact, '*liberales*', and the Spanish form of the word was used 'with the intention of suggesting that the principles of these politicians were unEnglish or akin to those of the continent'.[1]

This was ironical, since the word '*liberal*' had been adopted by the Spaniards for policies they regarded as *English*. The deputies who were called '*liberales*' in the Cortes were those who stood for the Lockean principles of constitutional monarchy and parliamentary government. Strange, therefore, that the British Tories should choose the name '*liberal*' to suggest something unEnglish. In the event their opponents were delighted with the name, since the word had acquired a laudatory emotive meaning in the sense of 'bountiful, generous, open-hearted'; the Tories' intended brickbat turned out to be a handsome gift.

The liberals were proud to admit that they believed in freedom. But freedom from what? The answer to that question must hold the key to the intelligibility of any sort of liberalism. The answer of the English liberal is unequivocal. By 'freedom' he means *freedom from the constraints of the state*.

Thomas Hobbes taught pessimistic resignation to absolute authority, but he gave his liberal critics a very clear statement of what is meant by 'the liberty of subjects':

> In cases where the sovereign has prescribed no rule, then the subject hath the liberty to do or forbear according to his own discretion.[2]

When the English liberal has advocated 'liberty', he, too, has

[1] O.E.D. '*Liberal*.' As late as 1816 Southey in the *Quarterly Review* wrote of '*liberales*'.
[2] *Leviathan*, chap. xxii.

thought of 'liberty to do or forbear according to his own discretion'. Elsewhere Hobbes specifies *the state* as the constraining factor when speaking of the liberty of subjects, and he expresses what is in fact a liberal principle with the apophthegm: 'The liberties of subjects depend on the silence of the law.'[1]

This is not to say the liberal accepts Hobbes's view that such liberties are a matter of luck—the gift of particular sovereigns, to be enjoyed where available but not otherwise to be demanded. The liberal *does* demand such liberties and demands them as rights. Nor must Hobbes's apophthegm be read too literally. He means that the liberties of the subjects depend on the silence only of those laws which constrain *subjects*. Some fortunate states have laws which constrain the executive government, and no one would suggest that the liberty of subjects depends on such laws as *these* being silent; on the contrary, their liberty is likely to be increased by such laws existing and being enforced. The English laws of *habeas corpus*, of bail, of police entry and arrest, all constrain or restrain the executive of the realm, and by so doing they increase the liberty of subjects.

It is arguable that the liberties of subjects do *not* depend on the silence even of those laws which constrain subjects, but to argue in this way is to argue *against* liberalism as liberalism is understood in England. For the 'liberty' on which English liberalism rests is, as we have seen, *liberty from the state*. Carried to an extreme form that principle of liberty would lead liberalism to anarchism. This, the English liberal has always recognized, and he has qualified his demand for the reduction of the constraints emanating from governments with the admission that there is a point beyond which they cannot be reduced—he accepts such constraints of the state as are necessary to ensure order within the realm, defence against foreign powers and the security of lawful possessions, the three principles Locke summarized as, 'life, liberty and property'.

In other words, English liberalism is the doctrine of the minimal state. And although much of its thinking is as old as the Stoics, the

---

[1] Chap. xiii. Some philosophers of absolute sovereignty have lacked Hobbes's simplicity and they have won a popularity he forfeited by giving a more noble and inspiring picture of the state and its institutions. Hegel, for example, alleged that 'Really every law is a liberty; for it contains a reasonable principle . . . which means . . . it embodies a liberty'. This may not be at variance with Locke's view that the law enlarges men's liberty, but it is a clear contradiction of Hobbes's view.

English liberal tradition is in many ways peculiarly national. John Stuart Mill remarked on this. The English, he said, had come to regard their liberty as something which had to be defended against governments. 'Continental' liberals, on the other hand, identified liberty with self-government, and held that people would be free if they governed themselves. I shall presently suggest that liberalism in continental Europe was not, even in Mill's time, one coherent doctrine; that there were, in fact, several continental liberalisms. But there was certainly one important continental variety of liberalism, deriving from Rousseau, which did, as Mill said, identify political liberty with self-rule, and on this basis went on to recommend the enlargement of the democratic state.

Mill disliked the thought of subservience to the democratic state because he disliked the thought of subservience to the will of the majority. He believed that the will of the majority was unlikely to coincide with the will of one particular man, especially of a cultured man. Mill was more afraid of the rule of the majority than some English liberals have been. Most English liberals, however, have wanted to minimize the power of representative governments no less than that of other sorts of government. One reason, indeed, why some nineteenth century English liberals favoured widening the suffrage lay in their belief, not altogether correct, that the more democratically a government was chosen the more moderate it would be.

To say that English liberalism is, to this extent, negative, is not to say that it has no positive side. It is simply that English liberalism, unlike certain foreign sorts of liberalism, looks for 'the positive' not in *freedom*, but in the qualities of individual persons. John Hallowell is right, so far as English liberalism is concerned, when he says: 'it is the political expression of an individualistic *Weltanschauung*',[1] although I think this is not true of nineteenth century German liberalism, which is primarily the subject of Hallowell's book. The English liberal has demanded freedom for the individual from the constraints of the state because he has regarded the invididual person as an ethical end, and the state as an instrument, of value only in so far as it could serve the interests of the individual person.

The English liberal has traditionally had, besides his moral view, an economic theory which has reinforced his belief in the minimal state. Liberals such as Locke and Mill, who were primarily philosophers,

---

[1] *The Decline of Liberalism as an Ideology* (Routledge, 1946 edition), p. 1.

have often been economists, too; and although there are differences among the many economists who are known as liberals, it was commonly held in the formative years of economic science and of liberalism alike that the economy of a community had its own laws of working, and that state interference in that process could only be deleterious. It was thus on scientific grounds that the early economists recommended the freedom for trade from the constraints of the state; by so doing they provided an empirical corollary to the liberal's ethical philosophy. Liberalism proclaimed freedom-from-the-state for the love of such freedom; the early economists argued (falsely according to many later economists) that trade and commerce worked to everyone's material advantage when it was free from those state controls that had been general in medieval times.

A distinction is often made in current English usage between a liberal and a Liberal. A Liberal is a supporter of the Liberal Party, and Liberalism is not so old as liberalism. The Liberal Party can certainly claim descent from the heterogeneous body of left-wing Whigs who were the '*liberales*' of 1815, but it is not necessary that a liberal should be a Liberal.

Liberalism (with a capital L) is whatever the Liberal Party stands for. The liberalism we are concerned with here is a wider, less definite philosophy. In the heyday of the Liberal Party, nearly every English liberal was also a Liberal. Such is no longer the case. English liberalism in the twentieth century has overflowed from the Liberal Party into the Conservative and Labour Parties, and it has always expressed the attitude of many non-party men; liberalism, more than any other creed, is 'the politics of the unpolitical'. A writer such as E. M. Forster, who has always been very sceptical in his attitude to politics, seems somehow a perfectly representative English liberal.

The Liberal has a Party programme. The liberal may have none beyond the simple demand for the minimal state, for freedom from the constraints of government; to say this is in effect to give a lexicographical definition of the word 'liberal' in the English language.

§

English liberalism has been remarkably successful, and even at the highest level of abstraction, success is not an inconsiderable factor. Historians have explained in some detail the conditions in which this success was achieved. Some have emphasized the Protestant Reformation, others the advent of capitalism; and although there is probably something to be said for both suggestions, there is probably even more to be said about the qualities of the British people which have enabled them to live orderly lives together without the constant intervention of their government. In places where the people have not such self-control, forbearance and initiative, the minimal state is impracticable and the absolute state is, as Hobbes believed, the only alternative to chaos.

Of course things have been easier for the English. Since the Norman conquest they have never known the rule of any government other than their own.[1] In pressing for freedom from the constraints of the state, the English liberal has not had to think about the constraints of an *alien* state. Few other liberals have been able, in the same way, to take their freedom from alien rule for granted; on the contrary, the chief preoccupation of liberalism as understood in many European countries has been with just such *national* freedom. Hence the common alliance of continental liberalisms and nationalism. English liberals have often been suspicious of nationalism, for fear of the *étatisme* which usually goes with it.

Today, English liberalism is less successful than it was. Less successful perhaps, because English liberals (with the conspicuous exception of Mill) have failed to agree about the importance of constraints *other* than those imposed by the state, from which men may demand to be free. Two such demands are of particular importance: the first for freedom from economic constraints, the second, for freedom from the constraints imposed by custom, morality, or the 'unwritten laws' of society.

The failure of nineteenth-century English liberals to see the importance of constraints arising from private economic power goes far to explain the later success of both socialism and reaction. A working man (or woman) in Victorian England was constrained in very few respects by Her Majesty's government. Yet that worker's opportunities for doing what he wanted would compare unfavourably with those of a slave in ancient Greece. He was constrained, and for all but a few hours of the day, by his employer. The alternative to accepting the

---

[1] Englishmen have seen the *threat* of such constraints, as in 1940, when the public hoardings were posted with the notice 'Your Freedom is in Danger'. The Communists were sardonically amused at this announcement being made by a government which was itself curtailing the civil liberties of Englishmen. (Had it not banned the *Daily Worker*?) But the 'freedom' in question and in danger was, of course, freedom from an *alien* rule.

rule of that employer—or another not unlike him—was starvation. Marx said that where the means of production are monopolized by the few, and the majority must work or starve, the employers are in a very real sense the *rulers*. They may exercise more power, constrain more people, and constrain them more completely, than the established government of the realm.

There is no point in denying the connection, in British political history, of the big employers with liberalism and especially with the Whig and Liberal parties. It has plainly been to the interest of the big employers to be unconstrained by governments in order that they might themselves constrain. Hence the familiar Marxist critique of liberalism. Looking for a means of limiting the power of employers to constrain them, many workers have seen hope for themselves in *increasing* the power of the state. Some workers have even wanted governments to eliminate existing employers and assume the employers' function. That demand is the highest common factor of the several sorts of socialism.

This is not to say that socialists are any wiser than liberals. For if liberals have been blind to the importance of constraints arising from the economic system, socialists have been no less blind to the constraints arising from governments not held radically in check. Some socialists have realized too late, what is now to be observed in the 'people's democracies' that to unite the government and the employers into one body is to concentrate new and terrible constraints against the subject who is also a worker. Obsessed with the situation of the proletariat in nineteenth-century industrial communities, socialists have assumed that the constraints which emanate from governments *do not matter* to the working-class; and for this reason they have said that 'liberal freedom' is a myth. The example of Eastern Europe has taught some socialists to moderate their contempt for liberalism—where they have still enjoyed the 'liberal freedom' of revising their opinions.

Some English liberals, in the meantime, have tried to incorporate certain socialist principles into liberalism. This has not been easy, since English liberalism calls for the limitation of the government's power, and socialism for more laws, more planning, and more controls. Yet some assimilation of socialism into liberalism is not wholly inconceivable. Liberalism is not anarchism. It accepts the constraints of the state in so far as they are necessary to liberate men from the more dire constraints of nature; there is no reason why it should not accept further constraints of the state in so far as they are necessary to liberate men

from the more dire constraints of the economic system, especially since
the 'economic science' of early liberals has been discredited.[1]

In practice, a liberal policy to which some measure of socialism has
been assimilated is not likely to work in any community unfamiliar
with the earlier and simpler kind of liberal rule. For while a liberal
system could be modified to accommodate some socialism, it is hard
to see how a totalitarian socialist society could be modified to accommodate liberalism.

The difficulty of assimilating some measure of socialism to liberalism,
is, moreover, small compared to the difficulty of maintaining a liberal
society *at all*. One of the lessons of Hobbes which is also a lesson of
history, is that the enjoyment of civil liberty and the minimal state is a
very rare experience for mankind. By far the greater number of human
societies have been ruled by absolute sovereigns. They are still. And
one of the lessons of Machiavelli, which history likewise reinforces, is
that a community accustomed to the rule of an absolute state cannot
easily learn to live without the constraints of such a system:

> How difficult it is for people living under a prince to preserve their
> liberty, should they by some accident acquire it as Rome did after
> the expulsion of the Tarquins, is shown by numerous examples
> which may be studied in historical records of ancient times. That
> there should be such a difficulty is reasonable; for such a people
> differs in no wise from a wild animal, which, though by nature
> fierce and accustomed to the woods, has been brought up in
> captivity and servitude, and is then loosed to roam the countryside
> at will, where, being unaccustomed to seeking its own food and
> discovering no place in which it can find refuge, it becomes the
> prey of the first comer who seeks to chain it up again.[2]

Together with constraints that derive from private economic power,
most liberals have overlooked the constraints imposed by social
custom and public opinion. John Stuart Mill was almost alone among
Victorian English liberals in his consciousness of their importance.
Early in his essay *On Liberty*, he writes:

[1] Mill himself moved towards the view that liberalism should assimilate
socialism; and L. T. Hobhouse, in his *Liberalism*, sets out in detail those claims of
socialism which he believes a liberal can and must accept. But Maynard Keynes
must be recognized as the most influential exponent of the theory of a 'mixed
economy', the marriage between liberalism and state control.

[2] N. Machiavelli, *Discorsi*, trans. L. J. Walker (London, 1950), I, 16, i.

When society is itself the tyrant—society collectively over the separate individuals who compose it—its means of tyrannizing are not restricted to the acts which it may do by the hands of its political functionaries. Society can and does execute its own mandates: and if it issues wrong mandates instead of right, or any mandates at all in things with which it ought not to meddle, it practises a social tyranny more formidable than many kinds of political oppression, since, though not usually upheld by such extreme penalties, it leaves fewer means of escape, penetrating much more deeply into the details of life, and enslaving the soul itself.

Protection therefore against the tyranny of the magistrate is not enough: there needs protection also against the tyranny of prevailing opinion and feeling; against the tendency of society to impose, by other means than civil penalties, its own ideas and practices as rules of conduct on those who dissent from them; to fetter the development, and, if possible, prevent the formation, of any individuality not in harmony with its ways, and to compel all characters to fashion themselves on the model of its own.

These are sympathetic sentiments, yet the suspicion lingers that some constraining power in public opinion is as necessary to the successful working of a society as the constraining power, however limited, of the state. It may even be true that a society can afford to limit the constraints of the state only to the extent that public opinion furnishes *alternative* constraints. In England, for example, the years of 'liberal ascendancy' in the half century or so before 1914 were years when public opinion was probably more severe and exacting than it had been at any other time in English history. In Germany, on the other hand, the constraining power of public opinion was at its weakest during the short life of the Weimar Republic between 1918 and 1933, which may well be one reason why the life of that minimal state was so short and the totalitarian reaction so spectacular.

The connection between Victorian liberalism and Victorian taboo—and by 'taboo' I mean all those social constraints to which Mill draws attention in the passage I have printed—points to an even older connection between English liberalism and Protestantism. Some historians suggest that liberalism 'derives' from the Protestant Reformation, and although there is nothing liberal in Luther's belief in uncritical acceptance of temporal authority and still less in Calvin's theocratic totalitarianism, the rather confused impact of the Reformation in England had doubtless some share in the birth of English liberalism. English Protestants had no one religious leader, and English Protestantism was thus, almost from the start, a sectarian movement. United, the Protestants of England might have been as intolerant as those of Massachusetts; divided, they had perforce to learn to put up with people who disagreed with them. Early English liberals, such as Milton and Locke, were strongly Protestant, and English liberalism generally stands in marked contrast to continental liberalisms in having maintained its links with Protestant, and even Puritan, religious movements.

The Liberal Party in pre-1914 parliaments leaned heavily on the Nonconformist vote, although by that time Nonconformity had ceased to be self-consciously political. In the eighteenth century, under the leadership of Price and Priestley, Nonconformists had made more noise with their demands for the Rights of Man than they made with evangelistic preaching, but Wesley converted Nonconformity into a movement of religious 'enthusiasts' who had no great zeal for the Rights of Man because they had no great hopes for life on earth. Yet Nonconformity was still effectively liberal because it was, after all, *nonconformity*. It opposed the pretensions of the Establishment and favoured the minimal state. The Victorian Nonconformist believed as intensely as any other liberal in freedom from the constraints of the government. What he did not believe in was freedom from the constraints of unwritten codes of conduct, of social pressures and taboo. It could scarcely have been otherwise. Under the Catholic Church priests had said what was right and wrong. According to Reformation teaching every man was to be a priest unto himself; which meant, in effect, that every man was a priest unto everybody else, and public opinion assumed sovereignty in morals.

G. K. Chesterton once said: 'The trouble with Nonconformists is that they are so conformist.' They had to be. Society, when it assumes the sacerdotal office, is a stern master. For society thinks and feels as a crowd, and therefore tends to think and feel more crudely, to enjoin more emphatically, to censure more stringently than a learned priest or bishop.

Conservatives have had reason to criticise liberalism. If liberalism helped to 'silence the law' it lent voice to the taboo. If it reduced the temporal powers of the bishops, it added to the spiritual powers of laymen. Truly it was a leading liberal, Mill, who protested at the 'tendency of society to impose, by means other than civil penalties, its own ideas and practices as rules of conduct for others', but the Non-conformist liberal element after the Industrial Revolution appreciably encouraged that tendency in England. It has always been a Tory, an Anglican, a Catholic principle that a man should obey Authority when Authority was vocal, but otherwise enjoy himself as his tastes inclined him. The Tory can therefore claim to have protected the subject's freedom against the proliferation of taboos. Was it not, for instance, King James I and later King Charles I who defended, against the Puritan magistrates, the freedom of the English people to play their games and drink their parish ales on Sundays?

Yet there is much to be said today in favour of English liberalism. If the state in nineteenth-century England was the source of relatively mild constraint, the twentieth century has seen its power increase a hundredfold; at the same time the constraints which originate in public opinion and private economic power have substantially diminished. In other words, the constraints on which the liberal has concentrated have become *more* important; the constraints he has neglected *less* important in the present century. It is therefore strange if it is true that liberalism has entered its 'decline' just when this altered balance of social constraints makes the liberal analysis more timely and correct than it was when it flourished in the years before 1914.

We have seen that English liberalism has the merit of a certain simplicity. Much as he may be criticized for concentrating exclusively on freedom from the constraints of the state, we are left in no doubt as to what an English liberal means by freedom. In England the word 'liberalism' is almost unambiguous. It is when we turn to a wider field that the full extent of the ambiguity of liberalism reveals itself.

2

FRENCH LIBERALISM

The ambiguity of liberalism is more marked in French than in any other European language. The explanation is largely historical.

1. Certain writers hold that as a result of events in France between 1685 (when Louis XIV banished the Protestants) and 1793 (when Louis XVI was executed in the name of liberty), the French people have been divided into two political camps, if not indeed two nations. One is the France of 1685 which supports the Catholic Church, royal prerogative, traditional social patterns, and the *Syllabus*; the other is the France of 1793, which opposes the Catholic Church and supports parliamentary government, social progress, and the Declaration of the Rights of Man. Such historians often call the one side '*royaliste*' and the other '*libéral*'.

We are told that the religious question holds the key to this division of France. Louis XIV deprived his country of all but one Christian institution, the Roman Catholic Church. Thus, unlike the English and Dutch and other peoples who could attach themselves to any of several denominations, the French had either to be Catholics or non-Christians. The *Weltanschauung* most attractive to non-Christians after the Renaissance was humanism, and France was effectively divided after 1685 into Catholics and anticlerical humanists. The Catholics, believing in original sin and the need for authority and discipline, favoured traditional political institutions (however imperfect); the humanists, believing that the happiness of men could be increased by intelligent effort, favoured political reform. From the division of France into Catholic and humanist there arose, we are told, the division of France into royalist and liberal.

A striking illustration of this analysis is provided by the Dreyfus case in the 1890s, which led the people of France to take up sides, passionately and bitterly, on an issue of one man's rights *versus* the honour of traditional institutions; behind Dreyfus, it is said, were the liberals, against him the royalists.

This two-nation analysis of France is not altogether discredited, but it has been shown to be deceptively simple. These critics admit the importance of the division of France into the Catholics and the anti-clericals, but they deny that all important political alignments can be explained on such a basis. They see not two but at least three continuing streams in French political thought. On the Right there is royalism and conservatism. On the Left there is the revolutionary stream, including extreme democratic theories, socialism, anarchism, syndicalism an Communism. There are disagreements among parties of the Right (The Right-wing *Action Française*, for example, was killed from the Right), and there are even greater disagreements among the parties of the Left. But between these forces of the Right and the Left, it is argued, there are those whose politics are moderate, owing something to both Right and Left perhaps, but upholding a tradition distinct from either. This is the Centre.

The interest to us of these rival interpretations is their use of the word '*libéral*'. The 'two-nations' school applies the word to all move-ments *not of the Right*; their critics apply the word '*libéral*' only to movements *of the Centre*. Thus on the 'two-nations' analysis *libéralisme* includes the creeds of the Left. On the other analysis *libéralisme* is a political doctrine at variance with the creeds of the Left.

2. The word '*libéral*' was not used in France in the eighteenth century, but there is no reason why we should not use it in describing the political movements of the time. Most historians, French and English alike, unfortunately use the word 'liberalism' indiscriminately to name two distinct political theories, each, on a fundamental issue, at odds with the other. I shall call these two French liberalisms (a) Lockean liberalism and (b) *étatiste* liberalism. The first derives from the teaching of Locke and the example of English constitutional practice since 1689. The second is the theory, largely inspired by Rousseau, which identifies political liberty with the democratic state.

French Lockean liberalism does not exactly resemble English liberalism. The principles of the Lockean settlement of 1689 are, if not as Balfour said 'the common property of all parties throughout the English-speaking parts of the world', at any rate the common property of the largest parties there. English liberals, as we have seen, are those who go *forward from* 1689 to further refinements of individualism. For the Lockean liberals of France, however, a constitutional settlement on Lockean lines was the *end*. It was the avowed end—avowed as far as censorship and cool self-love permitted—of Constant, Montesquieu and most of the Physiocrats. It is called 'liberalism' because it rests on a principle of liberty—liberty from the constraints of the state; and this is the essential principle it had in common with what the English know as liberalism.

This is also the essential principle on which Lockean liberalism differs from *étatiste* liberalism. *Étatiste* liberalism rests on a *positive* concept of liberty. The liberty of the individual should not, it is said by champions of this doctrine, merely mean *not* being ruled. It should mean that the individual rules himself. The *étatiste* liberal therefore urges the individual to make the state his own. Rather than minimize the state, as the Lockean advocates, the *étatiste* recommends remodelling it. Where the Lockean thinks of freedom as freedom from the state, the *étatiste* liberal sees freedom as something to be realized through the state. Where the working model for the one was the constitutional monarchy in England, the working model for the other was the *Landesgemeinde* cantons of Switzerland.

The *Landesgemeinde* is a method of direct democracy (still practised in Glarus, Appenzell and Unterwalden) whereby the citizens meet at intervals *en masse* to legislate for their cantons. It is a very old form of government, known to Tacitus, who called it a peculiarly Germanic institution (though similar institutions existed in ancient Greece). The *Landesgemeinde* have an advantage over parliamentary democracy on English lines: their laws are made by a majority of citizens, and therefore can be said to embody the will of the majority of citizens at the time they are passed, whereas under representative government, laws are made by a majority of *deputies*, and the will of the majority of deputies may well differ from the will of the majority of citizens. However, for better or worse, the *Landesgemeinde* are not practical models for the government of large nations. Ten thousand men may be gathered together in a stadium to legislate for a canton; but not ten or twenty million. Most Swiss cantons have abandoned their *Landesgemeinde* for representative institutions as they have grown. Glarus is the largest canton which has still a *Landesgemeinde*; its population is only 35,000. Even when Rousseau wrote, the population of France was already approaching 25,000,000.

But this impracticability of direct democracy in a large state is not the only objection to *étatiste* liberalism. There is another, more important one. *Étatiste* liberalism rests on a fallacy. For practical purposes this did not immediately matter, since the Age of Reason was going out as the Romantic Revival brought *étatiste* liberalism into fashion, but the fallacy is nevertheless there.

It can be seen in the argument on which *étatiste* liberalism bases its claim to be the politics of freedom, and this may be expressed in a simple syllogism: (1) The free individual is the individual who rules himself. (2) A democratic state is one through which the individual both rules and is ruled. (3) Hence, given a democratic state the individual is free. To this argument is added the corollary that since the democratic state ensures the individual's freedom, that freedom will not be furthered by reducing the power of the state but, on the contrary, may be furthered by *increasing* the power of the state.

The argument is fallacious because 'the individual' does not exist. What does exist is this and that and the other particular person, and under the most perfect democracy this and that and the other particular person does not rule himself. He is ruled by a body of which he is a member. He has, at best, a voice equal to others, but it is possible that one particular person may be outvoted on every particular issue that arises. It would probably be difficult to find any one individual citizen even in such a 'model democracy' as Glarus, for example, who approved of every decision that was taken by the majority.

The liberalism that was revived in France after the fall of Napoleon was Lockean liberalism. *Étatiste* liberalism had gone abroad, notably to Germany.[1] The word *libéral*, now becoming general in French use, was for a very few years unambiguous. It stood for the politics proclaimed by such men as Benjamin Constant. Though (like Rousseau) Swiss by birth, Constant based his politics on the example of England. He was staunchly Lockean:

> One must not build upon an abstract idea, in the illusory belief that it can increase the sum of individual liberty. . . . There is a part of human life which necessarily remains individual and independent, and has the right to stand outside all social control. Where the independent life of the individual begins, the jurisdiction of the sovereign ends. Rousseau failed to see this elementary truth, and the result of his error is that *Du Contrat Social*, so often invoked in favour of liberty, is the most formidable ally of all despotisms.[2]

Constant in Restoration France desired precisely what Locke had desired in (or in exile from) Restoration England. Constant and the other *libéraux* desired only to reproduce 1688 and 1689 in France. In

---

[1] When Mill spoke of 'continental liberalism' he referred to what I call *étatiste* liberalism.

[2] *Cours de Politique Constitutionelle* (Brussels, 1839), p. 64.

1830 they believed they had done so. Louis Philippe was enthroned in France on an understanding singularly like that on which William and Mary had been crowned in England. His accession was a triumph of the purest Lockean liberalism.

It also marked the end of liberalism's purity. Constant died in 1830 and his successors as exponents of liberal philosophy developed new and varying lines of thought. Tocqueville went to America and returned to France with a gospel of Jeffersonian liberalism which seemed more in tune with nineteenth-century ideas than Locke's; it was republican, where Lockean liberalism stood for constitutional monarchy; other writers favoured popular suffrage under the name of 'democracy' while Lockean liberalism shunned the name 'democracy' although it favoured representative institutions.

Events developed even more quickly than political theory. Politicians like Guizot who called themselves Liberals, and who were put in charge of the Kingdom of Louis Philippe, failed, not sensationally, but miserably. A new *bourgeoisie* basked in the liberty the Lockean state introduced; a stuffy, uncultured, money-grabbing trading class. The diminished state produced an increased Monsieur Prudhomme. The rest of France recoiled from the mediocrity of the *via media*. The rebellion came from the Left in 1848; the Right replied with Napoleon III. There has since been no Liberal party in France, few self-styled Liberals of any importance in French politics. When political Parties were formed later in the century, the name chosen by the Centre was not 'Liberal' but 'Republican'. This is not to say that liberalism died in France in 1848. Rather, the word '*libéralisme*' ceased then to call to the minds of the French any one political doctrine. Usage after 1848 gives no criterion for deciding who is a liberal and who is not. Inevitably we find in the political literature of the period references to a variety of different doctrines as '*libéralisme*'. Some writers leave their readers to speculate as to what they mean by '*libéralisme*', and it is a pleasure to turn to those who quarrel about the meaning of the word, even though such writers often fail to realize the nature of their disagreement. Thus, for example, we find Emile Faguet stimulating a controversy by expounding liberalism as the doctrine of the minimal state. 'The state', he writes, 'is an evil; a lesser evil than anarchy, but nevertheless, to be limited to the tasks of securing public order and safety through the justiciary, police and army.'[1] Beyond that, Faguet

[1] Emile Faguet, *Le Liberalisme* (Paris, 1912), p. 22.

says, liberalism recommends leaving all social activities to individual enterprise. His conception of liberalism reappears in the definition of the word *libéralisme* given in the 1935 edition of the *Dictionnaire de l'Académie Française*:

> Doctrine morale et philosophique qui réclame pour tous la liberté des opinions et la liberté de conscience.
>
> Il se dit aussi d'une Doctrine civile et politique suivant laquelle il faut donner aux citoyens le plus de libertés possible et le plus de garanties possible contre l'ingérence de l'Etat ou l'arbitraire du gouvernement.
>
> Il se dit également d'une Doctrine économique qui s'oppose aux théories protectionistes ou étatistes.

A French writer who attacks Faguet's exposition of liberalism (and by implication this dictionary's definition of the term) is Jean de Grandvilliers. He writes:[1]

> How the word 'liberalism' is perverted by those who treat it as synonymous with individualism! We must reply by giving the word 'liberal' its true sense.

Grandvilliers argues that a true liberal is one who seeks to extend public liberties, and that since the intervention of the state is useful and even necessary to achieve this end, a liberal will therefore encourage state intervention.

This dispute between Faguet and Grandvilliers has an oddly familiar ring. It is the old issue between Lockean liberalism and *étatiste* liberalism in a twentieth-century form. On the one hand there is the liberalism which is still based on individual freedom and on the other the liberalism which identifies liberty with popular self-government.

Our short investigation has shown that France has not, as England has, *one* liberal tradition. To that extent it is true that '*le libéralisme n'est pas français*'.[2] But French political thought is rich in *libéralismes*. Since there is no one kind of liberty, but many, it ought not to surprise us that France should have more than one kind of liberalism. The error would be to suppose when different Frenchmen speak of '*libéralisme*' that they mean, or ought to mean, the same thing.

---

[1] Jean de Grandvilliers, *Essai sur le libéralisme allemand* (Paris, 1914), p. 110.

[2] A point on which Faguet, an individualist, and the royalist Maurras agree. R. H. Soltau, *French Political Thought* (New Haven, Conn., 1931), p. 488.

3

GERMAN LIBERALISM

The word *'Liberal'* was first heard in Germany in 1812,[1] coming there, as it came to England, from Spain. In fact, Germans began talking of themselves as *'Liberalen'* just when they ceased to *be* liberals in the English (or the Spanish) sense. The last years of Napoleon's reign marked the end of the Lockean tradition of German liberalism and the beginning of a new one.

The old German tradition was not merely derivately Lockean; it had contributed much to the formulation of Locke's own thought. In the sixteenth century it was a German philosopher, Althusius, who proclaimed that sovereignty derived from the people; and it was the German *Naturrechts* school of jurists who provided the bridge between the Roman concept of *jus naturale* and the Lockean doctrine of natural rights.

The idea of natural rights is implicit in the concept of natural law. In Jacques Maritain's words, natural law does not 'prescribe merely things to be done and not to be done';[2] it also recognizes 'rights linked to the very nature of man'. The vital feature of natural law is that it is understood to be higher than positive law or 'the law of princes', and it provides a standard by which such law can be judged.

Natural law is at least as old as Stoic philosophy. Roman jurists made much of it, and in medieval Christendom it was not only recognized but upheld: it was identified with divine law, and a united Church was able to exert its formidable power to secure obedience to it. After the Renaissance it was the task of Grotius and his school to restate the doctrine in a modern, secularized form.

Through Pufendorf this doctrine of natural law and natural rights reached Locke, and became one foundation stone of his liberalism. Locke in turn influenced the eighteenth-century German liberals, among whom Wilhelm von Humboldt anticipated in 1791[3] several

---

[1] Jean de Grandvilliers, *Essai sur le libéralisme allemand*, p. 8.
[2] Jacques Maritain, *The Rights of Man* (London, 1944), p. 37.
[3] His book was not, however, printed until 1851.

refinements of liberalism later contributed to English thought by Mill. The very title of Humboldt's book *Ideen zu einem Versuch die Grenzen der Wirksamkeit des Staates zu bestimmen* reveals his preoccupation with limited sovereignty and the minimal state.

Humboldt argued there that the function of the state was not to do good, but to ward off evil, notably the evil which springs from man's disregard for his neighbours' rights. The State, he said, must 'not proceed a step further than is necessary for the mutual security of citizens and protection against foreign enemies; for no other object should it impose restriction on freedom'. He concluded that 'reason cannot desire for man any other condition than that in which each individual enjoys the most absolute freedom of developing himself by his own energies'.

Eighteenth-century Germany had also many liberal economists, including Kraus, for whom Smith's *Wealth of Nations* was the most important book after the Bible. But under the stresses of the French Revolution and the Romantic Revival, the Germans rejected their rich heritage of Lockean liberalism. They embraced several other sorts of liberalism, almost all of them *étatiste*, and *étatiste*, moreover, in a different sense from the French liberal school to which I have applied that epithet. For even the *étatiste* liberal in France was as we have seen, at heart an individualist. He believed in a strong state only in so far as it could be regarded as the individual's *own* state. The German liberals after 1812 dropped the individualism but kept the *étatisme*; not only because French experience had shown that individualism and *étatisme* make impossible partners, but because the German liberals had shifted their interest from the individual to the society as a whole. They were still concerned with the people, but they had come to view 'the people' as a national unit rather than a collection of separate human beings.

The leading movements for political change in Germany after the fall of Napoleon did not wish, as those of France had wished a generation before, to eliminate one old régime. They wished to introduce one new régime in the place of several old ones; a national state into which the German principalities should all be merged; nationalism did not merely influence their liberalism after 1812, it became the very essence of their liberalism.

There are circumstances in which the purest Lockean liberal might be a nationalist. If his country were subject to alien rule, one of his first moves towards the recovery of liberty would assuredly be to end that alien rule.

But in Germany after the fall of Napoleon there was no such question of ending alien rule. The unified German state was demanded for its own sake. One freedom the German liberal asked for was freedom from the several ruling princes, and he was not only willing but eager, to accept as the price of that freedom, subjection to an Emperor. This policy of rejecting a weak government in order to live under a powerful one is the antithesis of Lockean liberalism, and to the English mind there is something tragically absurd about the thought of the German liberals rattling from Frankfurt to Berlin in 1849 to offer the crown of All Germany to a Prussian monarch who detested liberalism, and who, in the event, grandly announced that he did not take crowns from commoners.

In return for the crown of All Germany the more naive liberals had hoped that Friedrich Wilhelm IV might have undergone a change of heart and assured his subjects their rights. But what rights? A Declaration of Rights inspired by German liberalism appeared in 1848. It differs significantly from the French Declaration of 1789. The French Declaration is essentially individualist; the German is dominated by the demand for national unity. The French proclaims the Rights of *Man*; the German the Rights of the *German People*.

The old teaching of Grotius and his school was subtly rewritten by the nineteenth-century German liberals. The foundation of the old liberalism was natural law and natural rights. The foundation of the new liberalism is the *Rechtstaat*. The principle of the *Rechtstaat* is said by a sympathetic foreign historian, Guido de Ruggiero, to consist in 'self-government, understood, not as the participation of the people in a legislative and governing parliament, but as the possession by local governing bodies of governmental function conferred by the general judiciary, administrative and financial laws of the State'.[1]

The difficulty of understanding in what sense German liberalism rested on a principle of freedom, is the difficulty of understanding what it was its votaries were demanding *freedom from*. For many German liberals it was not a question of freedom from anything. Here we must observe how nineteenth-century liberalism was reinforced by metaphysics. Simultaneously with the growth of German nationalism, German scholars were modernizing the Greek philosophers, notably Plato, with his notion of the state as a moral entity, an 'individual writ large', and Aristotle, with his yearning for a positive and moral

[1] *History of European Liberalism* (trans. R. G. Collingwood, Oxford, 1927), p. 254.

concept of freedom. Such a positive and moral concept of freedom the German metaphysicians supplied. Since it was a freedom which did not need to be freedom from anything, it conveniently filled the gap in the theoretical structure of German liberalism.

This positive concept of freedom is, of course, the product of processes examined in the first chapters of this essay. It is a philosopher's definition of freedom, at variance with the popular sense of the word. The definition has been well received. Two of the most distinguished historians of European liberalism, neither of them German, speak favourable of it.

Guido de Ruggiero writes:[1]

> The eternal glory of Kant is to have demonstrated that obedience to the moral law is freedom. Freedom thus coincides with the reality of the mind. . . . It is the spiritual energy which presides over, nourishes, and regulates all the activities of man. . . . As such, it is not restricted or atomically isolated within the narrow sphere of individual life. This would be the result of a merely negative freedom, tending to exclude all interferences from without, and to justify caprice. . . . It was the great merit of Hegel to have extracted from the Kantian identification of freedom with mind, the idea of an organic development of freedom, coinciding with the organization of society in its progressively higher and more spiritual forms. The historical experience of the nineteenth century had vindicated Hegel's view, by showing that freedom has the force of a bond capable of holding men together in associations the more lasting and fertile according as they are more spontaneous in their origin and autonomous in their choice of ends. . . . The State, the organ of coercion *par excellence* has become the highest expression of liberty.

John Hallowell approves of German metaphysical liberalism on ethical grounds; because it makes freedom not only positive but moral. In *The Decline of Liberalism as an Ideology*, he writes:[2]

> To an anarchic conception of society as composed of autonomous individual units, liberalism opposed the conception of an order transcending individuals, and placed the responsibility for realizing

[1] *Op. cit.*, p. 352.
[2] John Hallowell, *The Decline of Liberalism as an Ideology* (Berkely, Calif., 1943), p. 49.

this order, potentially embodied in eternal truths, upon individual reason and conscience.

The main argument of Hallowell's book is that German liberalism degenerated between 1848 and 1914 because of the influence of empiricism, which caused German liberals to cease to believe that freedom is a transcendant moral reality. This seems to me wide of the mark as historical analysis. A simpler explanation might be that German liberalism degenerated because its most prominent spokesmen in parliamentary politics were outwitted, compromised and finally demolished by Bismarck.

The German liberals never recovered from Friedrich Wilhelm's snub in 1849. Just as many French people turned away from Lockean liberalism after the failure of Louis-Philippe's constitutional monarchy and looked to the Left for leadership towards social change, so after 1849, did many German people turn from the liberals to the militarists of the Right for leadership towards national unity.

In September 1862 Bismarck made this memorable utterance:

> It is not the liberalism of Prussia which interests Germany. Prussia must reassemble and maintain forces for a favourable moment such as she has already once allowed to slip. It is not by discussion and the votes of majorities that the great questions of the time are settled. That was the great illusion of 1848 and 1849. Questions are settled by iron and blood.[1]

In the 1860s Bismarck's militarism flourished splendidly. Even liberals were impressed by it, and when Bismarck made conciliatory overtures to them, most of the Liberal deputies in the Prussian parliament promptly came to terms with him. After all, they were nationalists and so was Bismarck; why should they not join him? There were some German liberals who still felt that the gospel of the Rights of the German People divided them from the principle of Iron and Blood, but they were the minority. As it happened, neither the trimmers nor the independents prospered. In the Prussian chamber in 1849 there had been 279 parliamentary Liberals among 350 members. In the election of July 1866, when 'Iron and Blood' was at the height of its popularity, the Liberals lost half their seats. In the 1913 chamber of 443 members there were seventy-three National-Liberals and forty Independent Liberals.

[1] Grandvilliers, *op. cit.*, p. 83 (Author's translation).

Commenting on these figures, Jean de Grandvilliers writes:[1]

Le recul du Libéralisme en Allemagne depuis 1870 semble donc partout constant. N'est-ce-pas un fait surprenant, puisque dans le même laps de temps, et dans tout les États du monde, Angleterre ou Portugal, Espagne, Hollande. . . . il a, au contraire, progressé?

One answer is, of course, that the liberalism which was progressing in these other countries was a different doctrine. What was dying in Germany were various combination of constitutionalism and compromise, of bourgeois aspiration and metaphysical philosophy, of *Realpolitik* and the *Rechtstaat*.

But since 1918 the old Lockean liberalism has twice been revived in Germany, first in the Weimar Republic and for the second time in the West German Federal Republic. In the Weimar Republic German Liberalism sought to establish the pure doctrine of political *laissez-faire*; the Federal Republic has enthroned the pure doctrine of economic *laissez-faire*. To many liberals in England, where the doctrine of political *laissez-faire* has always been tempered by a deep belief in self-discipline, the Weimar Republic seemed *too* tolerant and morally weak, and events in 1933 proved those fears to be well founded. But so far the policy of economic *laissez-faire* has worked extraordinarily well in the Federal Republic.

---

[1] *Op. cit.*, p. 2.

4

AMERICAN LIBERALISM

In the United States the word 'liberal' has not the laudatory emotive meaning it enjoys in the United Kingdom. Neither has it the same descriptive meaning. When the word was first heard in British politics, America had been an independent republic for more than forty years, and was rapidly developing a political terminology of her own. American English was also in some ways more antiquated than the Regent's English. Words that had changed both descriptive and emotive meanings in England kept older associations in America. The older meaning of 'liberal', as Walter Skeat shows in his *Glossary of Tudor and Stuart Words* was 'licentious, gross' and the *Oxford English Dictionary* gives among its definitions: 'liberal—often used in the sixteenth and seventeenth century in a bad sense—unrestrained'. So Shakespeare used the word. When Desdemona, speaking of Iago, asks Cassio: 'Is he not a most profane and liberal counsellor?' she uses 'liberal' as a pejorative word.

Again there has never been in the United States, as in England, a Liberal Party.[1] We have distinguished the liberal from the Liberal— a member of the Liberal Party—but the existence of a party of people self-consciously *liberal*, has probably helped to sharpen the concept of liberalism in the English mind. Admittedly, America had a Liberal Republican Party, sometimes called the Liberal Party, for a year or two in the 1870s: but the kindest historian could not pretend that its members were united by any definite principles. They all disliked President Grant, and some of them disliked specifically his policy on tariff reform, the civil service and the South, but as Henry Watterson, an ardent Liberal Republican himself, observed, 'coherence was a missing ingredient'.[2] Horace Greeley, the Liberal Republican candidate for President, contrived to believe at once in Fourier-socialism, agrarian democracy, spiritualism, temperance and vegetarianism.

---

[1] The Liberal Party of New York is a State Party and not a national party.

[2] S. E. Morison and H. S. Commager, *The American Republic* (New York, 1950), vol. II, 70.

Though obviously a man of faith, he died three weeks after the Presidential election in which he was defeated, and the Liberal Republican movement died with him. The character of Horace Greeley caused many Americans to associate a 'liberal' with a visionary crank, and some still do.

Francis Otto Matthiessen wrote in 1948:[1]

> In our nineteenth-century political life we had no such formulated division as that between the Conservatives and Liberals in England. When the developing facts of our economy demanded some such division, the key-word seized upon by our native radical movement of the eighties and nineties, that of the Populists, was not 'liberal' but 'progressive'! That word kept its vitality through the time of La Follette and still possesses a core of traditional meaning from our political past. Such is not to be found in the borrowed and more washy 'liberal'. . . .

How, then, is one to explain the fact that in Vernon Louis Parrington's long unfinished history of American thought, published in 1927, the word 'liberal' occurs on almost every page?

Or should the question be, why did Parrington's pupil Henry Steele Commager never once use the words 'liberal' and 'liberalism' in his book *The American Mind*, published in 1950, although that book was intended to continue the study of American thought beyond the year 1900, where Parrington's book was cut short by his death?

Readers may remember that Lionel Trilling published in the same year as Commager's *The American Mind* a book of literary and social essays entitled *The Liberal Imagination*. Reviewing the English edition in a London paper, Raymond Mortimer wrote:[2]

> His use of the word 'liberal' must disconcert European readers. Liberalism suggests to us a passion for individual freedom and for toleration, and a corresponding distrust of organized power and its corrupting effect upon governments; but to him it implies, *inter alia*, 'a belief in planning and international co-operation, especially where Russia is in question.' In Marxism he appears to see, not the antithesis of liberalism, but its extension.

When Parrington wrote his *Main Currents of American Thought* the word 'liberal' was even more 'washy' than Matthiessen thought it in

[1] *From the Heart of Europe*, p. 90.
[2] *The Sunday Times*, 1 April 1951.

1948. Perhaps it was chosen—or as Matthiessen said 'borrowed'—precisely because it *was* 'washy'.

Main Currents of American Thought consists of three volumes, the last incomplete. Volume I expounds what Parrington calls the *first phase* of American liberalism. He writes:[1]

> The body of thought brought to America by the immigrant Puritans, and which gave a special cast to the New England mind, may be summed up in a phrase as Carolinian liberalism. It was the confused bequest of a hundred years of English idealism, struggling ... from the old static feudal order to the modern capitalistic; and it took a particular quality and received a narrow ideology from the current ecclesiastical disputes concerning the nature and government of the true church.

Although this earliest American liberalism was so much influenced by English precepts and achievements, it was significantly different. English liberalism was not *primarily* democratic. American liberalism was.

Indeed the *first* phase of American liberalism amounted to nothing other than a claim for democracy in church government and state government. Thomas Hooker, the liberal leader of Connecticut, once said:[2]

> It is also a truth that counsel should be sought from counsellors; but the question yet is, who should those be. Reserving smaller matters which fall in occasionally in common course to a lower counsel, in matters of greater importance which concern the common good, a general counsel chosen by all, I believe, under favour, most suitable to rule and most safe for relief of the whole.

Roger Williams, the free-thinker who persuaded a British Governor to give a parliamentary constitution to Rhode Island, put more emphasis on tolerance, as an English liberal might have done, but he too proclaimed democratic views long before experience of popular rule established the word 'democracy' so deeply in American hearts.

In fact, by the time of the French Revolution, Parrington says,[3] 'American liberalism had far outrun old-world liberalism and had

[1] Parrington, vol. I, p. 7.
[2] G. L. Walker, *Thomas Hooker* (New York, 1891), p. 122.
[3] Vol. I, p. 279.

produced an independent speculation of its own.' This marks its *second* phase.

'The doctrine of the diminished state, which was making persistent headway among English liberals,' Parrington writes, 'could make no appeal to those who desired an augmented state.'[1]

American liberals of this generation desired an augmented state for several reasons. Some arose from the peculiar condition of their nation, where authority was not altogether satisfactorily divided between the government of the Union and the governments of the several States. There was also the influence of Rousseau. Like many continental Europeans, the American liberals began to exalt government which was self-government and the state which embodied the people's will.

Briefly, Parrington's argument is this: from the birth of the American republic, two rival political philosophies contended for supremacy. Both could be called 'liberalism'. The first was 'the English philosophy of *laissez-faire*, based on the assured universality of the acquisitive instinct and postulating a social order answering the needs of the abstract "economic man", in which the state should function in the interests of trade'. The second liberalism derived from 'the humanitarianism of the French Enlightenment, based on the conception of human perfectibility and postulating as an objective an equalitarian democracy in which the political state should function as the servant to the common well-being'.[2]

In practice America adopted something much closer to the English liberal doctrine, both in the economic field ('freedom for trade') and the political ('freedom for subjects from the constraints of the state'). It is worth recalling in this connection a speech of Justice Brandeis:[3]

> [The makers of this nation] believed that freedom to think as you will and to speak as you think are means indispensable to the discovery and spread of political truth; that without free speech and assembly, discussion would be futile . . . they knew that order cannot be secured merely through fear of punishment for its infraction; that it is hazardous to discourage thought, hope and imagination; that fear breeds repression; that repression breeds hate; that hate menaces stable government; that the path of safety lies in the opportunity to discuss freely supposed grievances and

---

[1] Vol. I, p. 292.
[2] Vol. III, xxiii.
[3] Quoted by Morison and Commager in *The American Republic*, vol. II, p. 557.

proposed remedies; and that the fitting remedy for evil counsels is good ones. Believing in the power of reason as applied through public discussion, they eschewed silence coerced by law—the argument of force in its worst form. Recognizing the occasional tyrannies of governing majorities, they amended the constitution so that free speech and assembly should be guaranteed.

If this earlier kind of liberalism, with its emphasis on *laissez-faire* and tolerance, was more important in the *reality* of American political life, the second kind of liberalism provided the national political *mystique* and gave the words 'democracy' and 'liberty' and 'equality' something like the potency of spells.

With the twentieth century came what Parrington calls the *third phase* of American liberalism. This is the liberalism of the Left. Parrington is not without sympathy for it, but he has serious misgivings.

'Liberals whose hair is growing thin', he writes, 'are likely to find themselves in the unhappy predicament of being treated as mourners at their funerals.'[1]

Those liberals whose hair was growing thin in 1930 were liberals of the *second* phase, who believed 'that the cure for the evils of democracy was more democracy'. Liberals of the *third* phase believed that the evils of American democracy were too far gone for old-fashioned American democracy to cure. For the most part they looked to the stronger medicine of Socialism. They were all agreed that property must be subordinated to social justice. It was clear after 1900, Parrington writes, that American liberalism 'would either recede or pass over into radicalism. On the whole it followed the latter course'.

And 'radicalism' in the American language means something far more Left-wing and inflammatory than it does in English usage. Morison and Commager in *The American Republic*[2] include under the heading of 'radicals' not only Labour leaders, but Socialists, Communists, anarchists and pacifists.

Hence, however, 'washy' the word 'liberal', it has tended to be linked in American minds of the twentieth century with doctrines as extreme as these, and thus with doctrines sharply at variance with those the British understand as 'liberal'.

Matthiessen, when he called the word 'liberal' washy also said:

I am a socialist, though still without a party. The term 'liberal'

---

[1] Vol. III, p. 40.
[2] Vol. II, pp. 556–60.

seems entirely unsatisfactory now, since during the period of the New Deal it was given so many different senses as almost to rob it of its meaning. . . . [It] was used, I suspect, even by President Roosevelt himself, largely to render indefinitely free—and therefore as palatable as possible—some of the fundamental changes that he recognized to be essential in our economic system. The word has become increasingly weaker since Roosevelt's death because it is now a word on the defensive.[1]

'A word on the defensive.' It is this, perhaps, that holds the clue of Commager's rejection of Parrington's terminology. For it does not seem that he was motivated by any apprehension of ambiguity. Rather I suspect the explanation is connected with the changed emotive meaning of the word 'liberal' in the United States of America. In 1930 it was an 'aseptic' word. Since 1945, 'liberal' has become in many circles a *pejorative* word.

§

Parrington's successors drop 'liberal', and substitute, where they can, 'democratic' or 'progressive'. Now 'democracy' remains a laudatory word, and is unlikely to elicit from Americans, as it does from E. M. Forster, a model English liberal, a mere two cheers.[2]

Yet the word 'democracy'—as we see from Stevenson's illustration of emotive meaning—raises urgent problems of its own.

'Democracy' is, of course, a transliteration of the Greek word δημκρατία, itself a combination of δῆμος, the people, and κράτος, power. On this basis one might say that its descriptive meaning in English is simply 'rule by the people'. However, in the general usage of the Western world it has meant something more than this. It has meant the sort of system which admits more than one political party, so that a change of government without bloodshed is a practical possibility. But this conventional Western understanding of the word 'democracy' has been challenged. There is disagreement as to what 'democracy' means.

---

[1] *From the Heart of Europe*, p. 91.
[2] *Two Cheers for Democracy* (London, 1951). Forster gives democracy [in the modern Western sense] one cheer for admitting variety, one for permitting criticism. He withholds a third because democracy encourages the cult of mediocrity and fosters vulgarity by making mass approval the supreme arbiter. Like Mill, Forster believes there is a natural aristocracy of mind and taste and character.

There can be disagreement as to what democracy means partly
because there can be disagreement as to what δῆμος means. It may be
said that δῆμος means the 'people' but does not mean *everybody*.[1] The
old Southern States of North America could point to good Greek
precedent for the view that they were democracies although their
slaves had no vote, for there, as in the Greek republics, slaves did not
count as 'people'. Switzerland, often thought a perfect democracy, is
strictly a democracy only if women are not 'people', since in Switzerland women have no vote. The Republic of South Africa is likewise a
democracy, so long as the Black Africans are forgotten.

These examples of the flexibility of the word 'democracy' are no
longer the most embarrassing. The great international conflicts of the
contemporary world have been between those powers standing for the
principle of the one-party state and those powers opposed to that
principle. For a time, when the initiative of the totalitarian principle
rested with the Axis, there was no difficulty about describing that
conflict as totalitarianism *versus* democracy. This was because the
Axis powers agreed with their adversaries in the use of the word
'democracy'. They proclaimed themselves and their systems opposed
to democracy. When the totalitarian initiative passed to the Communists, there was no longer the old agreement about the meaning of
terms. The Communists proclaimed *themselves* democrats. They held—
and hold—that their species of totalitarianism is 'true' democracy. This
means that the word 'democracy' is now as ambiguous as 'liberalism'.

In the nineteenth century the word 'democracy' served usefully as
the name for the distinctively American style of government. Apart
from Switzerland, no other country in the world even claimed to be a
democracy. Since the end of the Second World War the situation has
come to be quite otherwise. Almost every nation in the world today
claims either to be a democracy or to be on the way towards becoming
a democracy. The word 'democracy' is universally exalted. Yet the
systems which claim to be democracies include systems as unlike as the
socialist totalitarian states of Eastern Europe and Asia, the populist

[1] Sir Ernest Barker, in his translation of Aristotle's *Politics* (1948 edition, p. 440)
writes: 'The word *demos* originally meant the countryside (*agros*), or the people
of the *agros*. By the fifth century B.C. it meant in Athens the whole Athenian community when assembled in the *ekklesia*. It may be identified with *to plethos* ("the
masses" or more exactly the *plenum*, or full body), and also with *hoi polloi* and
hoi pleiones ("the many" and "the majority"). It may also be identified with
ochlos ("the mob"), but this has a derogatory sense not conveyed by the other
words.'

nationalist regimes of former colonies such as Egypt and Zambia, no less than the parliamentary or representative systems of North America and North West Europe.

In this situation, the word 'democracy' has ceased to be an un-equivocal name for the type of government which is cherished by the majority of Americans. Just as the name 'liberal' has been, so to speak, captured and exploited in the United States itself by people whose political views are at variance with what was once understood as liberalism, exploited, that is, by various sections of the ideological Left in America, so in the world at large, the word 'democracy' has been seized and used by people whose views are sharply at odds with what Americans have traditionally understood as democracy.

The word 'progressive' has undergone in America similar meta-morphosis. F. O. Matthiessen, in the passage quoted above, mentioned 'progressive' as a key word in the native American radical movement of the late nineteenth century. In more recent times it has been put to use, in America and elsewhere, by Communists and other left-wing writers as a name for those persons who are well regarded from the Left. Thus, for example, those writers of the West who are found congenial behind the Iron Curtain, from Dickens and Zola to John Dos Passos and Arthur Miller, are dubbed 'progressive'. At the same time, the name 'progressive', like the name 'liberal', is favoured by American supporters of left-wing ideology as a less controversial-sounding name than 'socialist'. In the event, the more the word 'progressive' is used as a polite disguise for more extreme opinions the less does it serve as such a disguise; the disguise is penetrated and the word begins to acquire pejorative undertones. And it has then the unfortunate effect of drawing upon those whose views are avowedly liberal or progressive in an older and moderate sense the suspicion of entertaining views much more extreme than they do in fact entertain. What has happened is an illustration of the truth of the old proverb that bad money drives out good.

Part 3

THE FREEDOM OF THE WILL

1

IS THERE A PROBLEM OF
THE FREEDOM OF THE WILL?

The question of 'the freedom of the will' arose in Christian theology before it came in altered guise to enliven the less embittered controversies of secular philosophy. The Greeks were not concerned about it, although there is a discussion of 'free choice' in Book III of Aristotle's *Nicomachean Ethics*. St Augustine was, perhaps, the first to make it a living issue.

The problem of 'the freedom of the will' in Christian theology is that of reconciling two beliefs which seem to contradict one another: the first, that men can freely choose how to act; the second, that God is omniscient, and therefore knows in advance what every man will choose. Boethius states the problem thus:[1]

> If God beholdeth all things and cannot be deceived, that must inevitably follow which His Providence foreseeth to be to come; wherefore, if from Eternity He doth foreknow not only the deeds of men, but also their counsels and will, there can be no free will.

I am no theologian and cannot claim to know the answer to this riddle. Theologians who believe in free will have, however, resolved it in several ways. Some stress the point that God, to whom all things are possible, can both premove a man to choose a certain course and still allow him to choose it freely. Others suggest that God has several sorts of knowledge: '*simplex intelligentia*' or knowing what is possible; '*scientia visionis*' or knowing what is certain; and '*scientia media*' which is knowledge of what would occur if certain conditions were fulfilled. It is within the purview of God's *scientia media* that the will of man is said to be free. A Catholic author writes:[2]

> Acting now in the light of this *scientia media* with respect to

[1] Quoted by F. C. Copleston, s.j., *A History of Philosophy* (London, 1952), vol. II, p. 103.
[2] Michael Maher in *The Catholic Encyclopedia* (New York, 1909), vol. VI, 260.

human volitions, God freely decides according to His own wisdom
whether He shall supply the requisite conditions, including His
co-operation in the action, or abstain from so doing, and thus
render possible or prevent the realization of the event. In other
words, the infinite intelligence of God sees clearly what would
happen in any conceivable circumstances. He thus knows what
the free will of any creature will choose, if supplied with the
power of volition or choice and placed in any given circumstances.
He now decrees to supply the needed conditions, including His
concursus, or abstain from so doing. He thus holds complete
domination and control over our free actions, as well as over those
of a necessary character.

What I have called the 'issue' of the freedom of the will among
Christians is not, however, this problem of reconciling two beliefs
held by the same theologian, but a *dispute* between different theologians—between those who say that the will is free, and those who
put forward the doctrine of predestination.

The dispute is complicated by the fact that *both* views can be attri-
buted to St Augustine; and both parties claim to derive their doctrines
from him. St Augustine spoke of the human will as being free to do
right or wrong. He added that no man could do right by his own
efforts and his own strength. God's grace was needed. However, he
did not think God's grace was equally distributed; and in two works
written toward the end of his life, *On the Predestination of Saints* and *On
the Gifts of Perseverance*, he left the reader to conclude that there were
two sorts of people, those having God's grace, who could be saved;
and those without God's grace, who were damned from birth.

St Thomas Aquinas[1] is usually said by Catholic theologians to have
'reformulated' Augustine's teaching and presented a Christian
doctrine in favour of the freedom of the will. A leading Jesuit philosopher of the present generation, Father Frederic Copleston sums up
the Thomistic doctrine in these words:[2]

> That [man's will] is free follows from the fact that he is rational.
> . . . The reason, unlike instinct, is not determined in its judgment

---

[1] It is arguable, however, that a much more forthright case for the freedom of
the will is made by Albertus Magnus, notably in the 15th Tract of his *Summa
Theologiae*, where he holds that a man's free will can never be lost, even in a
state of sin.

[2] F. C. Copleston, *History of Philosophy* (London, 7 vols., 1952–60), vol. II.

concerning particular choices. Choice concerns the means to the final end (happiness), and it is possible for a man to consider it from more than one point of view. . . . *Liberum arbitrium* is the power by which a man is able to judge freely.

A denial of the freedom of the will was a leading feature of Reformation teaching. In opposition to Albertus Magnus and St Thomas, to Catholic teaching generally and (as it later appeared) to Anglican and even Wesleyan teaching, Reformation theologians held that man's will was rigidly predetermined in all its choices throughout life. In controversy with Erasmus, who defended the freedom of the will, Luther upheld predestination; and it was in reply to the *De Libero Arbitrio* of Erasmus that he wrote *De Servo Arbitrio*, rejoicing in man's slavery and helplessness. Calvin published an even sterner tract against the freedom of the will entitled *De aeterna Dei Praedestinatione*.

Calvin's argument had the merit of simplicity. All things sprang, he held, from the will of God; if a man's will were free, there would be another will beside that of God, and if this were so, things might arise which God had not ordained, and this would be to take the government of the world out of His hands, and leave it to chance and contingency. Calvin preferred to believe that the virtuous were virtuous because they had been elected by God and the wicked wicked because they had not been elected by God.

Calvin was pleased with his presentation of his case. It was not, he said, a 'subtle or thorny speculation . . . but a weighty argument, and excellently adapted to the furthering of piety . . . one which may well build up our faith [and] teach us humility'.[1]

But predestination, as argued by Calvin, raised other and still more disturbing difficulties. Even in Geneva, Calvin's biographer recalls, men were repelled by the suggestion

> that God should call all, yet elect only a few; that He should send His Son into the world to suffer an ignominious death for the purpose of saving those whose fate had been decided before the foundation of the world, and thus to effect a redemption by which nobody was redeemed; that He who is essentially just and merciful should consign one portion of His creation to eternal misery solely from caprice, or, at all events, for sins He would have necessitated them to commit.[2]

[1] Thomas H. Dyer, *Life of John Calvin* (1850), p. 265.
[2] Dyer, *op. cit.*, p. 261.

When Calvin was confronted with these difficulties, he would answer in the words of St Paul: 'Nay but, O man, who art thou that repliest unto God?' Such was the humility the doctrine of predestination had taught its author. Calvin's reply to the detailed and reasoned objections of Hieronymus Hermes Bolsec at Geneva in 1551 was to ask the Swiss Church to punish him with death. With the spread of Calvinist theology to other countries, belief in the freedom of the will became a dangerous opinion elsewhere, and it is on record that people went to prison for proclaiming it even in England, when England was a Puritan Commonwealth dedicated to the politics of freedom.

Safe as it has now become to criticize predestination, such is not to be the subject of our own enquiry. We shall look at the attack on the freedom of the will which is made by *determinism*, a doctrine which is a product of post-Renaissance science—predestination being, of course, a product of religion.

I have no doubt that 'determinism' could be defined in several ways, but I shall work on the definition given by its leading modern exponents. Determinism, thus defined, is the doctrine which asserts that everything which happens in the universe, including the actions and decisions of human beings, is in principle predictable. Opposed to this view is libertarianism, which asserts that some events, notably some actions and decisions of human beings, are *not* predictable in principle. The libertarian does not deny that some or even that many actions and decisions of human beings are predictable in principle (i.e. 'determined') he denies that *all* are.

It is these two views which are at issue on 'the problem of the freedom of the will' as I propose to discuss it in the remaining pages of this book.

§

It is fashionable to believe that this philosophical problem of the freedom of the will is a bogus problem, based on linguistic confusion. Such a view is not, however, new. Hobbes advanced it three hundred years ago in *Leviathan*. The antithesis of freedom and necessity, he there wrote, was a mistaken one.

> Liberty and necessity are consistent, as in the water that hath not only 'liberty' but a 'necessity' of descending by the channel; so likewise in the actions which men voluntary do, which, because they proceed from their will, proceed from 'liberty', and yet—

because every act of man's will, and every desire and inclination, proceedeth from some cause . . . proceed from 'necessity'.[1]

Hobbes added:

From the use of the word 'free-will' no liberty can be inferred of the will, desire, or inclination, but the liberty of the man, which consisteth in this, that he finds no stop in doing what he has the will, desire or inclination, to do.[2]

Locke took up this second point in his *Essay Concerning Human Understanding* of 1689, where he claimed[3] that the question whether a man's will be free or no is altogether improper; that it is a 'long-agitated' but 'unreasonable' question. On Locke's analysis, willing is one power, and liberty another, so that (§ 16)

to ask whether the will has freedom, is to ask whether one power has another power, one ability another ability; a question at first sight too grossly absurd to make a dispute or need an answer.

To ask whether the will is free is, Locke insists, to imply that the will is a substance or an agent, since only substances and agents can be free. He continues:[4]

The faculties have been spoken of and represented as so many distinct agents. For if being asked, what it was that digested the meat in our stomachs, it was a ready and very satisfactory answer to say that it was the *digestive faculty*. . . . And so in the mind, the *intellectual faculty*, or understanding, understood; and the *elective faculty*, or the will, willed or commanded. Which is in short to say the ability to digest, digested; and the ability to move, moved; and the ability to understand, understood.

Of course, it is not the *faculties*, he demonstrates, but a *man* who does these things.

Thus Locke is led to suggest:[5] 'The Question is not proper whether the *will* be free, but whether a *man* be free.' My objection to Locke's suggestion is that to ask whether a man is free may be to ask one of a thousand different questions—depending on what the man concerned

---

[1] *Leviathan*, chap. xxi.
[2] *Loc. cit.*
[3] Book II, chap. xxi, § 14.
[4] *Ibid.*, § 20.
[5] *Ibid.*, § 21.

might or might not be free from. Asking if a man is free from debt is
not the same as asking if a man is free from danger or prison or
engagements for the afternoon. To ask if the will is free is to ask
(however clumsily) quite a different question from any of these. You
can ask it without mentioning the word 'will'. Most people who uphold the freedom of the will would agree with Locke that there is no
such *thing* as the will. So he does not end the difficulty by proving
that what is not claimed to be a thing is not a thing.

Following Locke, several more attempts have been made to eliminate
the problem, but nobody seems to have worked along Locke's lines
until recent years. The chapter on 'The Will' in Gilbert Ryle's *The
Concept of Mind* is in harmony with much that he says, although Ryle
is more radical than Locke, and eliminates not only the will, but
volitions, too.

More immediately after Locke the attempt to eliminate the free will
problem was resumed on the lines laid down by Hobbes in the first of
his two arguments, namely that there was no genuine antithesis between
freedom and determinism. Such was the reasoning, notably, of Hume
when he wrote:[1]

> It will not require many words to prove that all mankind have
> ever agreed in the doctrine of liberty as well as in that of necessity,
> and that the whole dispute, in this respect also, has been hitherto
> merely verbal. For what is meant by liberty when applied to
> voluntary actions? We surely cannot mean that actions have so
> little connection with motives, inclinations and circumstances,
> that one does not follow with a certain degree of uniformity from
> the other, and that one affords no interference from which we can
> conclude the existence of the other. For these are plain acknow-
> ledged matters of fact. By liberty, then, we can only mean a
> power of acting or not acting according to the determinations of
> the will; that is, if we choose to remain at rest we may. Now
> this hypothetical liberty is universally admitted to belong to
> everyone who is not a prisoner and in chains. Here, then, is no
> subject of dispute.

Hume is saying in effect: (a) everyone who is not subject to external
constraints (e.g. chains, prison walls) is free, (b) the fact that human
behaviour is causally determined makes no difference to this freedom.
Therefore, (c) a man can be both free and determined.

[1] *Enquiry*, vIII, ii, 73.

Clearly, Hume is missing the point at issue. He proves that freedom from external constraints is compatible with determinism. But no one has ever doubted that it was. The dispute about the freedom of the will has nothing to do with freedom from or bondage to external constraints. The issue is this: the determinist claims that all our thoughts and doings are in principle predictable. Libertarians, upholding what they have called the freedom of the will, have maintained that *some* of our thoughts and doings are *not* in principle predictable. Hume fails to prove this dispute to be 'wholly verbal', because he fails to see that this is what the dispute of 'liberty and necessity' is.

A. J. Ayer is one of several writers of our own time who have followed Hobbes and Hume in arguing that the free will problem is a bogus problem on the grounds that there is no genuine antithesis between liberty and determinism. In an article contributed to *Polemic* 5, Ayer protests against the assumption that freedom is contrasted with causality and that a man cannot be said to be acting freely if his action is causally determined.

> For it is not [Ayer writes][1] *causality* that freedom is to be contrasted with, but *constraint*. . . . From the fact that my action is causally determined it does not necessarily follow that I am constrained to do it; and this is equivalent to saying that it does not necessarily follow that I am not free.

He goes on to say:

> If I am constrained I do not act freely. But in what circumstances can I legitimately be said to be constrained?

Ayer answers his question by giving as examples those situations: (1) in which a man holds a pistol to my head; (2) in which a man induces me to do what he wants by making it clear to me that, if I do not, he will create some situation that I regard as even more undesirable than the consequences of the action he wishes me to do; (3) in which another person has gained habitual ascendancy over me.

So far Ayer has gone no great way beyond Hume, and his argument is open to precisely those objections to which Hume's is open. However, Ayer does carry his argument an important step further. The constraints he considers are not only external constraints. He writes.[2]

---

[1] *Polemic* 5 (p. 41).
[2] *Loc. cit.*

It is not, however, necessary that constraint should take the form of subservience to another person. A kleptomaniac is not a free agent, in respect of his stealing, because he does not go through any process of deciding whether or not to steal. Or rather, if he does go through such a process, it is irrelevant to his behaviour. Whatever he resolved to do, he would steal all the same. And it is this that distinguishes him from the ordinary thief.

Later, in the same article, Ayer writes:[1]

> If I suffered from compulsion neurosis, so that I got up and walked across the room, whether I wanted to or not, or if I did so because somebody else compelled me, then I should not be acting freely. But if I do it now, I shall be acting freely, just because those conditions do not obtain; and the fact that my action may nevertheless have a cause is, from this point of view, irrelevant.

Ayer acknowledges, as Hume does not, that the question of the 'freedom of the will' is about something other than freedom from external constraints. He epitomizes the dispute as one concerning the truth of such a statement as 'I could have acted otherwise'. The main contention of the libertarian, Ayer says, is that such statements can be truly made. The determinist, on the other hand, is sometimes thought to deny that a man could truly say 'I could have acted otherwise'. Ayer suggests that the determinist need make no such denial. He continues:[2]

> To say that I could have acted otherwise is to say, first, that I should have acted otherwise if I had so chosen; secondly, that my action was voluntary in the sense in which the actions say of the kleptomaniac are not; and thirdly that nobody compelled me to choose as I did: and these three conditions may very well be fulfilled. When they are fulfilled, I may be said to have acted freely. But this is not to say it is a matter of chance that I acted as I did, or, in other words, that my action could not be explained. And that my actions should be capable of being explained is all that is required by the postulate of determinism.

Ayer uses the word 'explained' in this last sentence in the sense that entails 'predicted'.

---

[1] p. 42.
[2] p. 43.

We have now to consider whether this interesting argument proves what Ayer sets out to prove, namely that there is no antithesis between the libertarian claim and the postulate of determinism. I think he succeeds in reconciling the libertarian claim *as he states it* with the postulate of determinism. But I do not think he states the libertarian claim correctly.

People who uphold the freedom of the will maintain (according to Ayer) that it is possible for a man to say with truth: 'I could have acted otherwise.'

This, I suggest, is not enough. The libertarian claim entails that it is possible for a man to say with truth: 'I could have *chosen* or *decided* otherwise', in the sense of 'it was psychologically possible for me to have chosen or decided otherwise'.

This distinction is the subject of a discussion between Campbell Garnett and G. E. Moore in the American symposium entitled *The Philosophy of G. E. Moore*. In an essay published there, Garnett criticizes the view advanced in Moore's *Ethics* to the effect that moral responsibility 'merely means that (a person) could have done differently if he had chosen, without implying that he could have chosen differently'. Garnett maintains that a voluntary action is one in which a person has been able at one stage either to choose to or to choose not to perform it.[1]

In his Reply, published at the end of the same book,[2] Moore accepts this criticism. He writes:

> In *Ethics*, I thought that the mere fact that another action, which an agent *would* have done, if he had chosen, would have had better results than the action which he actually did do was *perhaps* sufficient to entitle us to say that the action which he did do was morally wrong.[3] I now think it is certainly not sufficient—a necessary condition for its being true that the action was morally wrong [i.e. also voluntary] is that he should have been *able to choose* some other action instead; if he *could not* have chosen any other action than the one he did choose, then his action cannot have been morally wrong [because not voluntary].

In his book *Ethics and Language*, Charles L. Stevenson gives a

[1] *The Philosophy of G. E. Moore*, ed. P. A. Schilpp (Evanston, Illinois, 1942), p. 181.
[2] *Ibid.*, p. 624.
[3] and thus voluntary.

definition of 'avoidable' which is very like the conditions of 'free will' specified by Moore in his original analysis and by Ayer in his *Polemic* article. Stevenson writes (p. 298):

> Let us . . . make clearer the meaning of avoidable by defining it in this way: 'A's action was avoidable' has the meaning 'If A had made a certain choice, which, in fact, he did not make, his action would not have occurred.'

On page 317 Stevenson writes:

> 'His action would have been different if he had chosen differently' . . . has the same meaning as 'His action was avoidable.'

D. J. O'Connor has reminded us in this connection[1] that:

> What we want to ask is: 'But was his *choice* avoidable?' And this question is necessary because it is choices and not actions that we praise or blame. Any action is praiseworthy or blameworthy only derivatively as being behavioural evidence of preceding choice.

The libertarian will not object to the suggestion that all our *actions* are, in some sense, caused, but only to the suggestion that all our *choices and decisions* are caused.

This matter is crucial. We ordinarily think of our choices and decisions as having reasons, as following upon deliberation, as based on considerations. Some of these considerations are general principles (for example: 'avoid lying', 'don't cause suffering', 'be polite'), some are calculations about the results that are likely to follow upon the several decisions that seem open to us.

Considerations of this kind result in our decisions, but considerations do not stand to decisions as causes to effects. In the words of a Harvard philosopher:

> An advocate of free will must admit that a volition is determined without a *cause*; but he does not need to assert that it is determined without a *reason*. Now, *motives* are reasons . . . and the relation between a reason and its consequent is often entirely distinct from that between a cause and its effect.[2]

If our decisions (or choices) *are* effects, they must have causes. Some

---

[1] *Proceedings of the Aristotelian Society* (1948).
[2] Francis Bowen, *Moral Philosophy* (New York, 1890), p. 298.

psychologists have seen the force of this simple point, and acknow-
ledging that premeditation cannot stand to decisions as causes to effects,
they have declared that the deliberation which precedes decisions is
irrelevant.

Sartre says it bluntly:

> Conscious deliberation is always faked. . . . When I deliberate
> the die is already cast. . . . The decision has been taken by the
> time the will intervenes, and the latter's function is simply to
> announce it.[1]

Clearly if decisions *are* effects, we must admit we are deceived in
thinking that we reach our choices as a result of consideration, or our
decisions through making up our minds. For, if every particular
choice is an effect, it could be shown to have followed, according to
some rule or other, from a given cause, and from the presence of that
cause the particular effect (the particular choice) could have been
predicted. Therefore a man could *not* truly say: 'I could have chosen
otherwise.'

For the moment, I am not judging the merits of the libertarian case.
I am trying only to state it correctly. Ayer, I have suggested, was
mistaken in supposing the libertarian claim sufficiently met if a man
could say with truth: 'I could have *acted* otherwise.' He goes on to
show that the determinist can agree to this, and thus to conclude that
there is no real problem at issue between the libertarian and the
determinist. I have argued that the libertarian claim is not sufficiently
met unless a man can say with truth: 'I could have *chosen* or *decided*
otherwise.' I have further argued that a determinist could *not* agree to
this, and that the issue between the libertarian and determinist therefore
remains.

§

A third argument for the view that there is no real antithesis between
the freedom of the will and determinism I take from a broadcast talk
by Patrick Nowell-Smith.[2] He argues that determinism is 'commonly
but erroneously supposed to deny the freedom of the will' because the
natural laws by which the determinist claims to explain the whole of

---

[1] J.-P. Sartre, *L'Étre et le Néant* (Paris, 1943), p. 527.
[2] An unpublished talk on the BBC Third Programme. Professor Nowell-
Smith has kindly lent me his script from which to quote.

human experience are misunderstood. Some people speak, he says, as if

> the laws of the solar system, for instance, are *rules* laid down by
> some Authority, which the planets are commanded to obey. . . .
> But the laws of science are not *rules*; they do not command or
> compel anything. They are descriptions of what planets actually
> do. And similarly, when a psychologist produces laws of human
> behaviour, he is describing how people actually behave, not
> ordering or forcing them to behave as they do. Being descriptions,
> the so-called 'laws' of science are quite unlike the laws of the
> state. For when a law of the state is broken it still remains a law;
> when a scientific law is broken, it ceases to be a law and becomes
> an exploded hypothesis. And for this reason, though I can disobey
> God's law or the moral law or the law of the state, nothing I can
> possibly do can possibly break a scientific law, and scientific laws
> in no way limit my freedom of action.

Nowell-Smith reminds us that this language of governing and
obedience is never taken seriously in physics. It can be used in natural
science only by forgetting its literal meaning. Nowell-Smith argues
that the entire free will controversy depends on taking it seriously in
psychology. He claims that there is a tendency to assume that if there
are psychological laws, they force or compel us to act as we do, just
as a policeman or a thug sometimes forces us to act against our will.
Hence people are apprehensive about the findings of psychology, and
are inclined to rebel against all attempts to discover laws of human
behaviour.

He continues:

> If I am literally *forced* to pull the trigger, I am not guilty of
> murder; it is true that where there is compulsion there is no
> responsibility. But the psychologist who believes that human
> action takes place according to laws does not believe that our
> actions are all forced on us in this way; he believes only that they
> are predictable. Any one who knows me well enough can predict
> how I will vote if there is a general election this week; but he
> does not thereby *compel* me to vote in this way. The fact of our
> action's being compelled and the fact of its being predictable
> are two quite different facts; and we only confuse them because
> we use this metaphor of governing, obedience and compulsion
> in our talk about scientific laws.

I believe that Nowell-Smith's argument[1] holds good against much that has been written in opposition to determinism, and that what he says about the nature of scientific laws is relevant to the question. But Nowell-Smith makes Hume's mistake. He contrasts freedom with coercion; he illustrates coercion by reference to a man being literally forced to pull a trigger. In proving that scientific laws do not compel, that predictability is not the same as coercion, he thinks he is proving that there is no antithesis between freewill and predictability. What does he do in fact? He eliminates not the problem itself, but the *language* of the problem. We have already seen Locke's early effort to end the difficulty about the freedom of the will by pointing out that there is no such thing as the *will*. Nowell-Smith in his turn eliminates the word 'free'.

It is worth observing here how the word 'free' comes into the dispute in the traditional formulation. There the question is put thus:

'Is all human experience subject to or free from scientific laws?'

Nowell-Smith says rightly that scientific laws are not the sort of things one can be subject to or free from. But we have seen that the traditional question can be reformulated without loss of meaning into the words:

'Are all human choices and decisions predictable?'

The word 'free' is removed; the question remains. Nowell-Smith's

[1] Nowell-Smith is not alone in making the point. It was made, for example, by Moritz Schlick in his *Problems of Ethics* (New York, 1939, chap. vii) which appeared in the original German in 1931 and in an English translation by David Rynin, published in New York in 1939. Schlick there argued that the 'bogus' problem of the freedom of the will derived from the ambiguity of the word 'law'. 'Law' may mean, as it does in the sense of civil law, something which *compels*. But 'law' may also mean, as it does in the case of a scientific law, something which *describes*. Now the principle of determinism or necessity only seeks to comprehend human behaviour under law in this second sense, under laws which *describe*. Since it does not wish to comprehend human behaviour under laws which *compel*, determinism does not limit freedom. The traditional problem of the freedom of the will, Schlick maintains, arises from the confusing of the two sorts of law, and the fallacious assumption that compulsion is an ingredient of law as such. I think this is a fair summary of Schlick's argument, although that is itself closely compressed in one short chapter of his book. The ambiguity of the word 'law' has been seen by several writers. As Kingsley Martin points out in *French Liberal Thought* (London, 1929, p. 127), Bentham noticed it in one of his attacks on Blackstone's *Commentaries* (see *A Comment on the Commentaries*, ed. Everett, p. 32). Schlick is therefore no more original than Nowell-Smith in making this point. Where he is original is in using it as the basis for 'eliminating' the problem of the freedom of the will. And where he is original he is, in my opinion, wrong.

attempt to eliminate the dispute has failed as Locke's failed because the free will question can be asked without using either the word 'free' or the word 'will'.

Ayer and Nowell-Smith hold that there is no antithesis between freedom and predictability. But the problem of the 'freedom of the will' is not a question of *freedom* versus *predictability*. It is simply the question whether our choices and decisions are predictable. If you can establish the case that our choices and decisions are predictable, you will 'eliminate the problem' only by conceding all that any clear-headed determinist has ever wanted.

As long ago as 1843, J. S. Mill wrote (*Logic*, ii, 416):

> Correctly conceived, the doctrine called Philosophical Necessity is simply this: that given the motives which are present to an individual's mind, and given likewise the character and disposition of the individual, the manner in which he will act may be unerringly inferred; that if we know the person thoroughly, and know all the inducements which are acting upon him, we could foretell his conduct with as much certainty as we can predict any physical event.

Predictability is all the determinist asks for; and total predictability is precisely what the libertarian will not concede.[1]

---

[1] Since writing this chapter I have read in *Mind* (LX, no. 240) an article by C. A. Campbell entitled 'Is "Free Will" a Pseudo-Problem?' which reaches much the same conclusion as my own. Following a close examination of Schlick's argument, Campbell decides 'it is an error to suppose that the "Free Will" problem, when correctly formulated turns out not to be a problem at all'.

2

SOLUTIONS

If there is, then, a genuine problem of the freedom of the will, if it has not been 'eliminated' the question next arises: is it soluble? Let us look at some philosophers' attempts to solve it.

First, Kant's. This has the advantage of being the work of a man no less interested in causality than in the freedom of the will. It is a complicated solution. Other philosophers have copied certain of its features, although few have given the question the prominence he gives it. In the *Critique of Pure Reason*, Kant sets before us the following antinomy:

> *Thesis:* Causality according to the laws of nature is not the only principle by which the phenomena of the world can be caused.
> *Antithesis:* There is no freedom, for everything in the world happens according to the laws of nature.[1]

Already in the Preface to the *Critique of Pure Reason*, Kant has adumbrated his solution of this antinomy. His method, briefly, is to divide the universe into phenomena and noumena. Determinism operates in the phenomenal realm, but not in the noumenal. Together with the rest of the universe, each human being has both phenomenal and noumenal existence. Thus Kant can say of one and the same man that his will is subject to the causality of nature and at the same time that his will is free from such causality; a man is determined as phenomenon but not determined in his supersensible, noumenal existence. Kant admits we have no *knowledge* of the noumenal person and cannot assert on theoretical grounds that it has free will. The possibility of free will transcends our power of understanding. The fact that it can be conceived without contradiction is, however, all important. For otherwise no arguments from the nature of moral consciousness could persuade us. From these considerations Kant derives his belief (and, he writes, 'I had to remove knowledge in order to make way for belief') that his philosophy of morals (entailing free

---

[1] *Critique of Pure Reason*, II, 2, ii, 2.

will) and his philosophy of nature (entailing determinism) can be developed, without conflict, each in accordance with its own laws.

In the *Grundlegung*, Kant defines the will as 'a mode of causality in living beings, in so far as they are rational'[1] and the freedom of the will is that quality of this (rational) causation 'by which it can work effects independently of foreign causes determining it'. Free will and rational autonomy are thus equivalent terms.

'What else then', asks Kant, 'is the freedom of the will but autonomy, that is, the property which the will has of being a law unto itself?'[2]

This does not mean that Kant uses the word 'autonomous' in the sense that some philosophers have used 'self-determining'. When he speaks of the freedom of the will he does not refer to the absence of external compulsion. In the *Critique of Practical Reason*,[3] Kant repudiates this suggestion firmly: 'Such freedom would be, at bottom, no better than the freedom of the turnspit; that, too, if once wound up, performs its movements of its own accord.'

Kant's moral teaching is thoroughly rational. To act reasonably, in his view, is to act morally. We have already seen that, on his analysis, to act freely is to act reasonably, for Kant is one of those philosophers who identify freedom with government by reason. It is not surprising, therefore, that Kant should have thought the freedom of the will and morality so closely connected that either could be deduced from the other.[4]

The connection is emphasized more than once in Kant's writings. In the *Grundlegung*[5] he says:

A free will and a will under moral law is identical, If, then, the freedom of the will is presupposed, morality with its own principles of freedom follows from freedom by mere analysis of its concept.

In the *Critique of Practical Reason*[6] he writes:

The two concepts are so inseparably united that practical freedom can also be defined as independence of the will of anything other than the moral law alone.

---

[1] Akademie edition, p. 416.
[2] *Op. cit.*, p. 447.
[3] Akademie edition, p. 97.
[4] A. C. Ewing, *Kant's Treatment of Causality* (London, 1924), p. 208.
[5] Akademie edition, p. 447.
[6] Akademie edition, p. 93.

How plausible is this solution? In the complexities of Kant's exposition it is easy to lose sight of a vital question, namely the question why
Kant insisted in the first place on the freedom of the will. His purpose
was to provide a basis for moral responsibility, for praise and blame.
'*Ought*', he says, 'implies *can*.' In other words, people cannot be
morally obliged to do what they cannot do; nor are people to be
blamed for having done what they could not help doing.

Several modern philosophers have questioned this conclusion, but
Kant certainly believed that the freedom of the will was a necessary
condition of moral praise and blame.

It is my belief that if we examine Kant's account of free will we shall
find that it cannot serve the purpose for which he intended it. Consider
the following points:

The free action, Kant says, is one that originates in noumenal
causation. But only *rational* action, only right actions, are thus
originated. Reason and morality are linked, *wechselbegriffe*. Only the
moral action is rational and only the rational action is free.

It follows that wrong actions, on Kant's theory, are not free, but
determined. And since determined actions are ones that could not have
been avoided, Kant puts himself in a position where he cannot blame a
man for acting wrongly. He cannot, that is, say a certain wrong action
should not have been done, because his theory puts all wrong actions
outside the realm of free will and into the realm of necessity.

True, he can say that *right* actions are free and therefore praiseworthy.
But nobody ever worries as to whether right actions are free or not
free. Only wrong actions give rise to *that* question. Gilbert Ryle, in
his *Concept of Mind* (p. 69) reminds us:

> In their most ordinary employment 'voluntary' and 'involuntary'
> are used, with a few minor elasticities, as adjectives applying to
> actions which ought not to be done. We discuss whether some-
> one's action was voluntary or not only when the action seems to
> have been his fault. He is accused of making a noise, and the guilt
> is his, if the action was voluntary, like laughing; he has successfully
> excused himself if he satisfies us that it was involuntary, like a
> sneeze. In the same way in ordinary life we raise questions of
> responsibility only when someone is charged or justly or unjustly
> with an offence. It makes sense, in this case, to ask whether a
> boy was responsible for breaking a window, but not whether he
> was responsible for finishing his homework in good time. We do

not ask if it was his fault that he got a long-division sum right, for to get a sum right is not a fault. . . .

In the ordinary sense, then, it is absurd to discuss whether satisfactory, correct or admirable performances are voluntary or involuntary.

This adds further to our criticisms of Kant. His doctrine of the freedom of the will not only leads to the conclusion that wrong actions are involuntary, and thus makes it illogical to blame or to administer retribution; but its major achievement—the identification of right actions as voluntary actions[1]—makes a point which, as Ryle shows was hardly in any case worth making. Even so I believe that Kant came closer to a solution of this problem than any other philosopher.

§

The second attempt to solve the problem of the freedom of the will which I propose to consider is that of a philosopher who is not nowadays much read—Henri Bergson; he deals with the subject at length in his book *Time and Free Will*.

Bergson is interested in Kant's treatment, and criticism of Kant makes the scaffolding for the exposition of his own ideas. Bergson attacks the 'two-world' solution. He accuses Kant of making freedom of the utmost importance and then escorting it, with due ceremony, up to a sort of 'noumenal' attic where it will not be in the way.

When we assert the freedom of the will, Bergson says, we assert that the relation of the (freely willed) action to the state from which it issued cannot be expressed by a law. Admittedly psychologists presuppose that the same motives acting afresh on the same person would again produce the same effect. Psychologists do so, and are permitted to do so, because we are not accustomed to observing ourselves directly, but only through forms borrowed from the external world. Intellectual thought, and particularly the language of communication, can itself become a falsifying process, since it reduces to simple and like terms that which is essentially complex and dissimilar. Indeed, the farther we

---

[1] H. J. Paton, in *The Categorical Imperative* (London, 1947), dismisses this reading of Kant as mistaken. He suggests that Kant *does* suppose a man to be free when he acts wrongly. There are yet other ways of reading Kant. W. T. Jones, *Morality and Freedom in Kant* (London, 1940), sets out several possible interpretations.

probe into ourselves the more do we find that our states of consciousness permeate and melt into one another, and each becomes tinged
with the colouring of the others. Language has often only one word
for these infinitely various states. Thus, Bergson concludes, it is an
inaccurate psychology, misled by language, which shows us the human
personality as governed by scientific laws.

So far, it seems to me, Bergson's case is fairly plausible; although I
must admit to having simplified—even over-simplified it—by leaving
out of account the tortuous theory of time to which Bergson himself
repeatedly refers. We now pass to a part which is less readily convincing.

He asserts that a personality is a unitary whole—not an aggregate of
conscious states. The outward manifestation of this inner, unitary self
is precisely what is called a 'free act', since the self alone will have been
the author of it, and since the act will express the whole of the self.
The freedom of the will admits of degrees; an act is the more free, the
more it is a man's own; the most free act is therefore the *creative* act.

The self often develops a spatial, superficial or social crust. It is
possible that conscious expression should go no deeper. Many people
live entirely at this level, and thus never acquire the freedom of their
will. On the other hand, if the whole soul assimilates experience, a
man's actions will be an expression—a creative expression—of his
unique inner self. A man may either live passively and be determined,
or live creatively and enjoy freedom of the will.

Bergson denies that the question about the freedom of the will is
about the capacity of human beings to make particular choices between
alternatives. If the question is put in these terms, he says, the victory
in the dispute will always go to the determinists. The common idea
of the moral dilemma, of 'the man at the cross roads', he considers
misleading. What he thinks happens when a man hesitates between
two alternatives is that he passes through a series of states tending the
one way or the other, all the while building up an ever expanding and
changing self. Hence there are not really two contrary states, but a
large number of successive and different states within which a man
distinguishes by an effort of imagination two possible directions. The
self lives and develops until the free action 'drops from it like an over-
ripe fruit'. That last metaphor is typical of Bergson's vivid style.

Bergson's style is, indeed, rather too vivid. The reader is more and
more stimulated, but less and less convinced. For consider:

1. Bergson accuses Kant of bifurcating the self, and pushing freedom
out of the way into a 'noumenal attic'. Yet Bergson does something

very similar himself. He develops a theory of a superficial self (which is determined) and an inner self (which enjoys free will).

2. Bergson seems sometimes to be saying that a free act is no more than an agent's own act. We have met this assertion before, and noticed something wrong. It rests on the mistaken idea that the question of the freedom of the will is about 'freedom' in general, and not, as it is in fact, about the predictability of human choices and actions. The antithesis is between determinism and something not altogether happily called 'the freedom *of the will*'. To say that an act is *my own* is to say nothing about whether it is determined or not. It is perhaps to say it is self-determined. But that is not the sense of the word 'determined' here at issue. The word 'determined' is used in this controversy to mean 'predictable'. To say that an action is *my own* is to say nothing at all about its predictability.

3. Bergson's description of the free act as the creative act seems to rest on a tacit redefinition of the word 'free'.

Concerning this third criticism of Bergson's case, I have certain misgivings which will become clear in a later chapter. I shall suggest that while the 'creative act' is not the logical equivalent of the 'free act' (which I take to be Bergson's view), the 'creative act' is one important kind of demonstrably unpredictable act.

§

Modern readers of the *Nicomachean Ethics* are sometimes disappointed that Aristotle should have raised the problem of the freedom of the will and then not come to grips with it. Aristotle says that good deeds are done by men of good character and that doing good deeds gives a man a good character. Likewise with bad deeds. On this view a man who has done wrong might say: 'I couldn't help it: I am only acting in character when I behave in that way.' Aristotle's reply would be that a man *can* help having the character he has.

Can a man help having the character he has? His earliest actions shape his character. But his earliest actions are done when he is a child and hardly knows what he does. The responsibility for the child's character belongs to the parents. These parents, too, had parents, who were responsible for the first formation of *their* character, and so on backwards in time to Adam.

Aristotle's own writings offer no resolution of this familiar dilemma. A modern writer who has inherited the problem and tried to solve it is John Wisdom. His solution is found in *Problems of Mind and Matter*, an early book, written before he became Professor of Philosophy at Cambridge and before his association with Ludwig Wittgenstein had 'cured' him of metaphysical perplexity. The young John Wisdom was still interested in the problem of blame. He believed that we must establish the freedom of the will as a precondition of blame, but that we must also maintain the principle of universal causation according to which everything that happens and has happened since the first event in history is determined. He writes (p. 118):

> What blame requires is that however far we go back in setting out the causes of your act, we shall never come to a time at which a set of purely external circumstances, i.e. not involving you and your will, formed a complete cause of your act.

Thus, if you are to be blamed for anything, the causes of the causes of the causes of your decisions, however far back they may be pushed in time must include the determination of your will by your will. But time goes back to the beginning of the world, Very well, says John Wisdom, then your *self* must go back to the beginning of the world. You must have somehow existed before you were born. And why not? Oriental philosophers are for the most part of this opinion. Why should we, on account of Western prejudice, exclude the possibility?

An article in *Analysis* (vol. 3, no. 3) by Helen Smith demonstrates the futility of John Wisdom's curious Hindoo holiday. For pre-existence to help in the difficulty of blame and free will, she shows it would be necessary for people to *know* that they had lived other and earlier lives. People do not in fact know anything of the kind. Helen Smith concludes:

> If judgments of blame imply pre-existence, [John Wisdom's argument] goes to show, *not* that we have pre-existed, but that we are never justified in attributing blame.

§

Another Cambridge thinker unhorsed by a woman critic while riding high in the belief that he had rescued ethics from the menace of determinism was Arthur Eddington. His critic was Susan Stebbing.

Both the views of Eddington and the mistakes of Eddington are too well known to need detailed repetition here. Briefly, Eddington used the discovery of a measure of unpredictability in sub-atomic physics as the basis for asserting that physical events were not determined. From this he went on to say that since science was no longer 'deterministic', there was no longer a conflict of free will *versus* determinism. Determinism had been defeated—or rather withdrawn from the ring by its sponsors, the scientists. The libertarians had therefore triumphed. Heisenberg's Uncertainty Principle, which Eddington called tendentiously the Indeterminacy Principle,[1] was said to have 'opened the door to human freedom'.[2] Eddington[3] said: 'I think there is no longer any need to doubt our intuition of free will . . . our purposes, our volitions are genuine.'

Of this last remark, Stebbing[4] asks:

> How can the Principle of Uncertainty assure us that our purposes and volitions are *genuine*? What can be meant by saying that we need not any *longer* doubt our intuition of free will?

Stebbing asks Eddington to consider what would happen if Einstein were successful in re-establishing strict predictability as the basis of physics. Would that lead Eddington to doubt his intuition of free will?

> Assuredly not [she writes]. How then can the results of the work of physicists have any bearing upon this intuition?

Stebbing points out that twentieth-century developments in sub-atomic physics have a very limited significance for scientific method. Science generally is as 'determinist' as ever in the sense that prediction in fields other than the sub-atomic is still in principle possible. The predictability or unpredictability of human behaviour is not affected by the 'loss' of predictability from sub-atomic physics, for human behaviour is not the subject which is studied in sub-atomic physics.

Again, Eddington held that because certainty in science was 'now replaced' by high probability, the freedom of the will was no longer in jeopardy.[5] But no scientist who has chosen his words carefully, at any rate since Hume's *Treatise* appeared in 1739, can have claimed more than high probability for his laws and predictions. The only difference since Bohr and Heisenberg is that even this high probability is seen to

[1] See *Proc. Aris. Soc.*, Supplement IX.
[2] A. C. Eddington, *New Pathways in Science* (Cambridge, 1935), p. 88.
[3] A. C. Eddington, *Science and Religion* (London, 1929), p. 126.
[4] L. S. Stebbing, *Philosophy and the Physicists* (London, 1937), p. 218.
[5] See *Philosophy and the Physicists*, p. 213.

be in principle unattainable in certain clearly defined areas of sub-atomic physics. Thus we see that science has *not* 'repudiated determinism' and that the conflict of the freedom of the will *versus* determinism has not, as Eddington imagined, thereby ended in favour of the libertarian.

§

A further attempt at a solution to this problem is one based on the dual assertion that determinism is a methodological assumption of science to which we give *intellectual assent* while the freedom of the will is something we *feel*. It is said that, although the two are at variance, we can hold them simultaneously because they are based on different sorts of knowledge.

This seems to be the argument of a paper contributed by Paul Weiss to *Ethics*.[1] Once more we meet bifurcation. We have been offered two worlds, two selves, and now we are offered two sorts of knowledge. This latest is perhaps the most plausible dichotomy, for very few of us would wish to argue that there is only *one* sort of knowledge. Indeed, I think the difficulty in the way of accepting this solution is not so much the bifurcation as the second of the two premises: that the freedom of the will is something we *feel*. The word 'feel' is here used to mean some sort of intuitive belief reinforced by a sense of certainty. Sometimes the word '*know*' (suitably underlined) is used instead of 'feel'.

I have already quoted a reference by Eddington to an 'intuition' of free will.[2] Paul Weiss uses these words:

> In the very act of choosing, we are aware that we could have done otherwise. It is because and so far as we *know* this, that we *know* we are free.[3]

Brisker affirmations on the subject are Dr Samuel Johnson's celebrated words: 'Sir, we *know* the will is free, and there's an end on't,' and a similar remark by R. B. Braithwaite at an Aristotelian Society meeting in 1931:[4]

[1] Vol. LII, p. 186.
[2] *Science and Religion*, p. 126.
[3] *Ethics*, LII, p. 186.
[4] *Proc. Aris. Soc.*, Supplementary vol X, p. 196.

As for the pure philosophical 'freedom of the will,' my will is as free as I feel it to be and there is an end of the matter.

One would not wish to deny that Samuel Johnson and Arthur Eddington had intuitions of free will or that Paul Weiss and R. B. Braithwaite still have them. But clearly it is not everybody who has this inner certainty of the freedom of the will or there would otherwise be no sincere believer in predestination or determinism. In fact there have been very many believers in both those doctrines, and it would be outrageous to suggest that they were all insincere.

In a case where some people have an intuitive certainty and others do not, the question still remains as to which is the true belief. And even if we admitted the doctrine—which God forbid—that feelings are more reliable sources of knowledge than intelligence, this feeling of free will would only reinforce the case against determinism if *everybody* felt it, in which event, the case for determinism would never have been seriously argued.

Do many people in fact have a feeling of free will? Of this one may well be doubtful. What we *do* have is the *feeling of freedom*. I have discussed in the first part of this essay the feeling we sometimes have that we are *unconstrained*, and subject to no pressure in reaching our decision. A person who is sometimes subject to neurotic compulsion may possibly have a special feeling on those occasions when his decisions are *not* subject to neurotic compulsion. But this would be neither a feeling nor an 'intuition' of the freedom of the will, and it is probably only thought to be such because of the unfortunate use of the term 'human freedom' to describe both the absence of constraint or burdens *and* the freedom of the will.

Secondly, we sometimes have a sense of agency, a sense of being the cause of things. Such is the feeling from which some theorists have suggested we get our idea of causality—the wrong idea of causality, incidentally, if it is meant to be the analogue of causality as understood by scientists—and which differentiates our active experience from our passive experience. It is perhaps this consciousness of agency which has been described as a feeling or intuition that the will is free. Yet while it is true that I am certain that it is I (and nobody else) who dip this pen into the ink-well, I have no certainty that the action was unpredictable. I suspect that Paul Weiss and the others have again been misled by the language of the problem into confusing the self-determined act with the unpredictable act.

Nevertheless I think there is something to be said for Paul Weiss's suggestion. When we look back on decisions or choices we have made fairly recently, and can remember all the thoughts we had before we finally made up our mind, we can recall the experience of deciding. Thinking of that experience of deciding, we may say 'I *know* it was touch and go, because I *remember* how near I was to *another* decision'.

The difficulty, and it is one to which I shall return, is this: the belief that I might have come to another decision diminishes with time and distance. I believe I could have decided differently yesterday, but I am not so sure that I could have decided differently when I think of a decision I made twenty years ago; or that another person can help choosing as he does choose.

§

In the previous chapter we examined the view that the problem of the freedom of the will is a pseudo-problem, and we found reasons for rejecting that view. In the present chapter we have considered the attempts of several philosophers who acknowledge the problem to be a genuine one, to solve it. The results have not been encouraging. We have arrived at the point where we started. We have still found no way of reconciling belief in the freedom of the will with the common assumption of scientists that everything in the universe is in principle predictable. But can we sustain this state of doubt? What, we are likely to be asked by people who want to force a conclusion on us, about ethics? The question is a relevant one, and my next chapter will attempt to meet it.

3

ETHICS

The connection between ethics and the problems of the freedom of the will is readily seen. It is widely held that the freedom of the will is a necessary condition of ethical judgments being made or, at least, appropriately made. Kant said: 'Ought implies can', and we might all agree that praise and blame are equally illogical, when there is no responsibility for the actions which excite the one and provoke the other.

The connection with ethics was discerned by theologians when the problems of the freedom of the will was *their* problem, and predestination the doctrine to which the libertarian was opposed. Among the teachings of Christianity are these: (1) that God created the universe, including human beings; (2) that some human beings are wicked; (3) that God is both omniscient and omnipotent. The doctrine of the freedom of the will enables Christian theologians to attribute the wickedness of men to men. God, they could say, gave men the choice of being good or evil when He gave them the power of choosing, or gave them free will. Theologians who denied free will and advocated predestination, could not, it was said, attribute the wickedness of men to men. On their view a man's sins were inevitable. And if a man's sins were inevitable, then the man who committed them could say he 'couldn't help' committing them. If he 'couldn't help' committing them, it was surely absurd to blame him. The sinner could shift the blame on to the Creator, pointing out that his particular sin was part of the divinely ordered pattern of history. The original author of human wickedness must then be God Himself, and God should be blamed for each man's sins.

Scientific determinism has no such impieties among its implications. But it is still linked to the question of blame. If predestination leads to blaming God instead of sinners, scientific determinism seems, as we have already observed, to require us to stop blaming altogether. And just as people resisted predestination because they did not want to blame God, so do people resist scientific determinism because they do want to blame sinners, or as they might prefer to say, to reproach and punish those who violate the ethical codes of the societies they live in.

In my opinion, predestination *does* entail blaming God for each man's sins. I am not sure that if scientific determinism were true it would follow that we could not, in some sense, blame people for doing wrong. We should have to abandon blaming them, if determinism eliminated the distinction between involuntary and voluntary actions, by making all actions involuntary. But determinists deny that they do so. Some determinists have offered a basis for distinguishing between voluntary and involuntary actions, in the light of which the notion of blame need only be *revised*, not eliminated.

The nineteenth-century utilitarian, Sidgwick, wrote in his *Methods of Ethics*:[1]

> The determinist can give the fundamental terms of ethics perfectly clear and definite meanings. The distinctions thus obtained give us a practically sufficient basis for criminal law; while the moral sentiments actually existing are seen to be appropriate and useful, as part of the natural adaptation of social man to his conditions of life. The determinist allows that, in a sense, 'ought' implies 'can'; that a man is only morally bound to do what is 'in his power'; and that only acts from which a man 'could have abstained' are proper subjects of punishment or moral condemnation. But he explains 'can' and 'in his power' to imply only the absence of all insuperable obstacles *except* want of sufficient motive.

Later philosophers of the analytic school have improved on this argument in several interesting ways. Two well-known essays in the field are Charles L. Stevenson's chapter on 'Avoidability and Indeterminism' in his book *Ethics and Language* and Patrick Nowell-Smith's article 'Freewill and Moral Responsibility', in *Mind*.[2]

Stevenson's treatment is connected with the so-called 'emotive' theory' of ethics he expounds in the earlier chapters of his book.

> Although [he writes, p. 302] we all of us make judgments and influence attitudes for mingled, complicated purposes, a part of our purpose, and usually an essential part, is to control how people will subsequently act.

Ethical judgments, on this view, look mainly to future actions.

[1] H. Sidgwick, *Methods of Ethics*, 6th edn. (London, 1901), chap. v.
[2] *Mind*, vol LVII, no. 225 (Jan. 1948), p. 55.

What we blame or praise is always an action done, and therefore past; but we speak the words with a view to affecting future actions; we want to discourage actions of the sort blamed and to encourage those of the sort praised. However, not all actions *can* be modified. Judgments often induce men to give money to charity, but never make men add a cubit to their stature. Since we are unwilling to talk aimlessly we confine our judgments to actions of the first sort; to those actions which judgments are likely to modify. It is only the sort of actions that Stevenson calls *avoidable* which can be modified by ethical judgments. He defines an 'avoidable' action as 'one that would not have occurred if the agent had not made a certain choice'. To say an action is avoidable is, on this view, to say nothing about whether that *choice* was determined or not.

> Reformative and preventive theories [Stevenson writes, p. 306] have long made clear that punishment of unavoidable acts would fail to serve an important purpose. All that has been overlooked is that ethical judgments, being quasi-imperative, have also a reformative and preventive function.

It is because it is *impossible* to control unavoidable actions that we are unwilling to make such actions the subject of ethical judgment. We hesitate to judge actions over which control is *very difficult*. But as it becomes easier to control actions, our willingness to judge tends progressively to increase. Stevenson gives the example of a man addicted to opium. In the early stages of his addiction we judge him, since our judgment may serve as a means of deterring him. When he is further on in the habit, we no longer judge but use other means of stopping him.

> Although the avoidability of an act [Stevenson continues, p. 312] . . . is usually considered a necessary condition of its being judged, many other conditions are often necessary as well. Yet avoidability remains a consideration that is of particular interest.

Nowell-Smith develops a similar argument without the special use of the word 'avoidable', stressing instead the distinction between 'voluntary' and 'involuntary' actions. He makes his case in the context of the following logical framework:

(*a*) Value judgments apply only to events (including their consequences), but not to their causes (*b*) Events that are 'good' or 'bad' constitute moral actions only when they are caused by someone's voluntary decision.

(*c*) 'Good' and 'bad' events that are also moral actions are fit subjects for praise and blame, while other good and bad events are not.

(*d*) This 'fittingness' is a causal relation discoverable ... by reflection and experience.[1]

Nowell-Smith points out that moral actions are a sub-class of good and bad acts. A moral action is also one that can fittingly be praised or blamed, and Nowell-Smith believes it to follow from this that a moral action is one that *can be brought about or prevented* by praise and blame. This suggests a rule for deciding which classes of actions are voluntary and which are involuntary. Voluntary actions are simply those which *can* be influenced—encouraged or discouraged—by praise and blame. The falling of stones is not discouraged by praise and blame. Neither are the actions of the insane or of compulsive neurotics. These are involuntary actions.

Nowell-Smith is not only advising us to praise, blame and punish where praise, blame and punishment work; he is offering the *effectiveness* of praise, blame and punishment as a *criterion* of voluntary as opposed to involuntary action.

§

If Nowell-Smith is right, determinism does not 'make ethics go by the board' or make praise and blame absurd. It simply substitutes *pragmatic* blame for 'backward-looking' blame (together with reformative and deterrent punishment for retributive punishment).

In other words, Nowell-Smith has shown *how* the determinist can (as Sidgwick said he could) 'give the fundamental terms of ethics perfectly clear and definite meanings'. I know of no better method than Nowell-Smith's by which the determinist can do so. And it is in some ways a very attractive method. It allows us to praise and blame where praise and blame are *effective* instead of where praise and blame are *deserved*, and since we are never sure about deserts, this change of policy has much to recommend it.

Nevertheless two serious difficulties obtrude themselves. Nowell-Smith's analysis of moral responsibility appears to carry the following implications:

[1] *Mind*, LVII, 225, p. 55.

1. Since blame and punishment *does not* affect the behaviour of the hardened criminal, the hardened criminal cannot be said to be morally responsible for his misdeeds.

2. Since punishment *does* affect the behaviour of many cats and dogs and other animals, many cats and dogs and other animals must be said to be morally responsible for their misdeeds.

It is doubtful whether either of these propositions would be generally acceptable, for both conflict with the common notion of what moral responsibility is. And while Nowell-Smith has successfully shown that determinism is consistent with ethical judgments, it is consistent only with ethical judgments of a strange, strained kind. It would be rash to suggest that the universal desire to make ethical judgments is a sufficient ground for rejecting determinism. On the other hand, the libertarian can certainly give a more 'common sense' (if not a more true) justification of the moral judgments we make.

§

There is more to be said about the *pragmatic* distinction between voluntary and involuntary action, and the difficulty there is in finding a *real* one. The distinction between voluntary and involuntary action has interested philosophers since the time of Aristotle. Aristotle defined voluntary actions as 'that of which the originator is the agent, he being aware of the particular details in which the action consists'.[1] Involuntary action is 'of two kinds, being done either on compulsion or by reason of ignorance'.[2] Aristotle may not command our agreement here, since most of us take the view that the distinction between voluntary and involuntary actions is neither primarily nor secondarily a distinction between knowledge and ignorance; but between actions done on purpose and those done under duress or accidentally or automatically.

Some peculiar things have been said in this connection. Ayer and others have used the example of the difference between the kleptomaniac and the thief to illustrate the difference between involuntary and voluntary agents. Here one may find oneself asking—what is this supposedly illuminating distinction? In English criminal law the actions of the insane are recognized as involuntary and punishment is withheld in favour of 'treatment'. But insanity is defined by a set of

---

[1] *Nicomachean Ethics*, chap. iii, § 3.
[2] *Loc. cit.*, §1.

rules laid down by the Law Lords in 1843, before the birth of modern
psychological medicine. Are we to accept these as a reliable guide? It
is sometimes said that an intelligent jury can be relied on to decide
whether a prisoner is responsible for his actions. Yet we often read of
cases where juries look to professional psychiatrists as expert witnesses
to guide them, because they, the jurymen, think they do not know
enough about psychology to settle the matter for themselves (although
the law leaves the final decision on the question to them). What is
more, we often read of cases where two professional psychiatrists report
contrary findings: one that the prisoner *is*, the other he is *not* 'responsible' for what he has done.

It might seem easy enough to point to an example of a kleptomaniac: a millionairess lately afflicted with sleepy sickness caught
abstracting articles of no value from popular stores. Equally, an
example of a thief: a skilled safebreaker filling a sack at midnight in a
jeweller's vaults. But suppose the safebreaker is sent to a Freudian
analyst, who reports that the man was deprived of maternal love in
infancy and brought up in circumstances which made the illicit
acquisition of jewellery a neurotic compulsion? Is he not then properly
to be called a *kleptomaniac*?[1] Let us suppose too that our millionairess
is unfortunate enough to come before an unenlightened magistrate.
She is committed for a time to prison, and thereafter never again
possesses herself of other people's property. This will surely suggest to
Nowell-Smith that she was a *thief* after all. Punishment has succeeded,
and so on his analysis, she must have been 'to blame'.

The truth is, I believe, that the law is the wrong quarter in which to
look for help. The law does not *want* a watertight criterion for distinguishing the voluntary offender from the involuntary. For the law
is not ass enough to imperil the social machinery it governs by adopting
rules which might well lead to the identification of *almost* every
criminal offence as an involuntary one.[2] Legal penalties today are

[1] Since writing this, I find that the point was made by George Eliot in 1872 in
her novel *Middlemarch* (chap. 23): 'When a youthful nobleman steals jewellery
we call the act kleptomania, speak of it with a philosophical smile, and never
think of his being sent to a house of correction as if he were a ragged boy who had
stolen turnips.'

[2] Stuart Hampshire in his book *Spinoza* (Harmondsworth, 1951, p. 151) makes
the point that 'as our psychological and physiological knowledge of human
actions and reactions increases, the range of human actions of which we can
reasonably say "an alternative action was possible", or "he could have acted
otherwise", necessarily diminishes'.

expected to serve two purposes besides, if not instead of, that of retribution: to reform the offender and to deter the rest of us from following his example. Between these two purposes there is an unfortunate contradiction: to reform the offender the authorities must (psychologists tell them) be *kind* to him;[1] to deter the rest of us, the authorities must make us believe that if we follow the prisoner's example, they will inflict pain on us. Therefore, since reform and deterrence cannot be accomplished by the same method, the law has to improvise and compromise, to act irrationally. The situation might be met by some immense deception whereby the public was led to believe that conviction was followed by unpleasantness while, in fact and in secret, conviction was followed by genial and kindly therapy. Failing such deception, the law can afford to reform only a few of its prisoners; the majority must be punished as an example to the rest of us. Hence the law will make this first demand of its criterion of involuntary offences—that only a minority of offences shall come within the reach of it. The trend of psychology and physiology is towards the view that the majority of offences are involuntary. That is why the law sticks to its old-fashioned definitions. The law does not want to know the truth if the truth is going to upset the social order it is designed to secure. Is it not therefore strange that philosophers should look to criminal law for guidance in their doubts?

[1] A former British Lord Chief Justice, Lord Goddard, as reported in *The Observer* (22 April 1951) said at a national conference of Probation Officers: 'There is a craze for sending children to psychiatrists to-day and I think it is absolutely wrong.

'Most approved schools will tell you that you can usually tell boys who have been sent to psychiatrists. They are cocky and self-assured because they think they are interesting cases.

'I have come away from a visit to an approved school wondering why my father bothered to send me to a preparatory school. Some of them are far more comfortable than my prep. school was.'

4

PREDICTION

So far I have tried to establish these positions:

1. That the problem of the freedom of the will is not a pseudo-problem.

2. That the determinist can find a place for blame and moral responsibility in his theory, by giving a special pragmatic analysis of blame and moral responsibility. The pragmatic analysis, however, strains credence too far in respect of at least one of its implications. If the libertarian is correct, a much more acceptable analysis of moral responsibility is possible; one could say 'Ought implies can' without giving any peculiar account of 'ought' and of 'can'.

3. That the distinction between voluntary and involuntary action is one the determinist seems unable satisfactorily to explain.

We shall now consider the question into which the old question: Is the will free?' resolves itself, namely 'Are human choices and actions wholly predictable?'

First let us investigate how the determinist reaches his affirmative reply. Certain steps can be traced in the process:[1]

1. In many branches of science we have no occasion to question the postulate of induction that the future will be like the past. We predict, on the basis of previous observations, for example, that a certain chemical solution of known ingredients will turn red litmus paper blue.

2. We then extend this sort of prediction to much more complicated processes; for example, to the behaviour of a rat in a maze. This leads us to believe that the behaviour of rats can be predicted with a high degree of probability; and from this we are led to think that if we knew *everything* about the rat (having all the information which our present instruments and methods cannot yield), then we could predict the behaviour of the rat on any given occasion or at any given moment with perfect certainty.

[1] I am indebted to the late Professor John Hartland-Swann for several suggestions incorporated in this chapter.

3. This process prompts the scientifically minded person to apply the same reasoning to man himself. Modern research in genetics, physiology, neurology, to say nothing of the less exact sciences of anthropology, sociology and psychology has shown that a man's behaviour is *largely* predictable or, as some might say, 'determined by' his genetic constitution, social environment, glandular secretions, and so on. What is particularly striking is the evidence which suggests that many people's 'moral decisions' are predictable. (The evidence, for example, of Lange's[1] study of identical twins.)

4. The next step in the development of the determinist position follows easily. From the success of these sciences, it is supposed that if *all* the predisposing factors were known, then it would be possible to predict *exactly* what a man would do or decide on any given occasion or at any given moment.

The weakness in this train of reasoning will be found at stage (4). We have no justification for proceeding from the discovery that *some* kinds of human behaviour are predictable in practice to the belief that the *whole* of human behaviour is predictable in principle; from the discovery that some parts of the human organism function in a machine-like way to the belief that the *whole* human organism is a sort of highly organized machine. Ryle has forcefully attacked this 'para-mechanical' hypothesis.

He has also reminded us that

> Whenever a new science achieves its first big successes, its enthusiastic acolytes always fancy that all questions are now soluble by extension of its methods of solving its questions. At one time theorists imagined that the whole world was nothing more than a complex of geometrical figures, at another that the whole

[1] 'Some years ago Professor Lange, with the help of the Bavarian Ministry of Justice, investigated every available case in which a person who had come into contact with the police was a member of a pair of living twins of the same sex. His object was to discover whether the other member of the pair of twins had a criminal record; whether, in fact, the likelihood of criminality in one member of a pair of twins was greater, if criminality existed in the other. So far as ordinary twins were concerned, the additional likelihood appeared to be very small. . . . In the case of pairs of identical twins, however, the position was very different. Thirteen pairs were investigated where one member of each was a criminal, and in ten cases the other member of the pair was found to be a criminal. What is more, there was a marked similarity between the crimes of which criminal pairs of twins were convicted.' C. E. M. Joad, *Guide to the Philosophy of Morals and Politics* (London, 1938), p. 235.

world was describable and explicable in the propositions of pure arithmetic. Chemical, electrical, Darwinian and Freudian cosmogonies also enjoyed their bright but brief days. . . . The physical sciences launched by Copernicus, Galileo, Newton, and Boyle secured a longer and stronger hold upon their cosmogony-builders than did either their fore-runners or their successors. People still tend to treat laws of Mechanics not merely as the ideal type of scientific laws, but as, in some sense, the ultimate laws of Nature.[1]

Ryle adds one of his characteristic apophthegms: 'Men are not machines, nor even ghost-ridden machines. They are men—a tautology which is sometimes worth remembering.'[2]

It is true that people's behaviour is frequently predictable. We are more often right than wrong in our estimates as to what others will do and decide. But from the fact that we are *often* right on the strength of *incomplete* information it does not follow that we could *always* be right if we were better equipped.

There are, indeed, very good reasons for denying the possibility of absolutely accurate prediction (on scientific lines) of men's actions and decisions. Let us consider some of them.

It may be useful to distinguish three kinds of prediction. The first I shall call 'predictions about you', the second 'predictions about myself', the third 'predictions about other people'. The first two kinds of predictions are those made to the knowledge of the people about whom they are made. And that is a factor of the utmost importance.

Imagine we are playing billards together. I have left the balls in a position very favourable to you. I watch you take up your cue to play your stroke. Perhaps I say to myself: 'He will pot the red.' You do, and my prediction is verified. Perhaps, on the other hand, I do not keep my prediction to myself. I say aloud: 'You'll pot the red.' This very utterance may well have the effect[3] of putting you off your stroke. *Because* I have said to you: 'You'll pot the red' you *don't* pot the red. I am now told that my prediction was 'incomplete' because I did not include in that prediction a calculation of the consequences of making that prediction known. Suppose I had extended the prediction in this

---

[1] G. Ryle, *The Concept of Mind* (London, 1949), p. 76.

[2] *Op. cit.*, p. 81.

[3] See Stephen Potter, *Gamesmanship* (London, 1947).

way; I should then have had to tell you: 'You'll pot the red, but because I've said so you won't pot the red.' The effect of this extended
prediction may be quite different from the effect of announcing the
original prediction. Many players find that a prediction that they will
not succeed in a manoeuvre is much less apt to put them off their stroke
than a prediction that they will succeed in their manoeuvre. Let us
suppose that you are such a player. The result of my extended prediction 'You will pot the red, but because I've said so you won't pot the
red' is that after all you *do* pot the red.

If there is this difficulty in predicting (to you) your actions, how
much the more difficult must it be to predict (to you) your choices.
Imagine I have a friend who is parsimonious. If I said to him: 'You
won't give a Christmas box at the club this year', he might take my
words as an accusation of meanness, and promptly, in an attempt to
disprove this allegation, hand a five pound note to the porter at the
club. Likewise a don may say to his best pupil: 'You will excel in the
examinations' and to his worst pupil: 'You will probably fail.' The
effect of the words on the very good pupil may be to give him too
much confidence, cause him to relax in his preparation for the examination, and finally to do badly; the effect of the prediction on the very
poor pupil may be to sting him to new efforts with the result that the
result is quite good. Yet another example is provided by the Gallup
Polls. If the Gallup Poll predicts that seventy per cent of the electorate
will vote for the Right, the effect of reading this prediction on a
'floating voter', who had said he would vote Right on the assumption
that the Left was too strong, might be to make him revise his decision
and vote Left, since the Gallup Poll has now shown the Right to be
much stronger than the Left. In the event, it is quite possible that merely
by announcing its prediction of a seventy per cent right-wing vote
the Gallup organization reduces the right-wing vote to sixty per
cent.

In each of these instances the predictions announced might well
have been correct if they had been kept secret. My parsimonious
friend would have given no Christmas box; the bright pupil would
have come high in the examination and the dull one have failed; and
right-wing parties would have received seventy per cent of the vote.
It is not enough to say that the predictions should have been extended
to include the effects of making them known. For every time I extend or
modify a prediction I make to you about you to take account of the
consequences of making that prediction known to you, I am making a

fresh prediction which may have consequences different from those of
the preceding prediction, and a prediction yet further extended to
take account of these altered consequences may itself have different
consequences . . . and so on without end.

That is why predictions made *to you about you* are impossible. But
what about my predictions about myself? Here we meet the same
difficulty. My conduct is repeatedly affected by the predictions I make
about myself. But for a *scientific* prediction, I must make a calculus
which takes into account the consequences of all the predictions I make
about myself; that calculus must therefore take into account the prediction which it is supposed to furnish. Thus I can never complete the
calculus. And thus I can never make a satisfactory prediction to myself
about myself.

My third sort of predictions I have called 'predictions about other
people'. By this I mean predictions about somebody who does not
know the prediction I am making. I predict, but I do not tell him what
I predict. Therefore the factors which frustrated predictions about you
and predictions about myself do not now arise. In such cases as this one
can certainly envisage the possibility of success. For here we have
something like laboratory conditions. Is it not conceivable that one
day scientific techniques will have reached the point where everything
about a man at present unknown or concealed will be *observable*, and
as a result of being observable, ultimately predictable?

There are flaws in this picture. By definition 'prediction' means
saying before. To predict an event you must say it *will* happen, not that
it is happening or has happened. And some events, by their nature,
must elude prediction. Consider this example:

At a certain point of time in 1816, the poet Keats composed his
verses on autumn beginning with the line: 'Season of mists and mellow
fruitfulness'.

Poets are not good at explaining how they do their work; but there
is one thing we can be sure of. Part of the business of making up a line
of verse is saying that line of verse silently or aloud. The poet does not
think it out and then say it to himself. Saying it to himself is part of
thinking it out, or making it up.

To predict that Keats would compose the line—'Season of mists and
mellow fruitfulness'—the psychologist would have to observe all the
factors involved in making it up, all the process that led to its composi-
tion. But the poet's utterance of that line to himself is one of those
factors, part of that process. Therefore the observer would not have

all his material until the line had been said, until it was, so to speak, made up. Thus he could not predict it because he could not say it was going to happen before it happened.

We may take also the example of an invention. The date is not recorded, but let us suppose that the corkscrew was invented at ten p.m. on 1 March 1650. Now if it were possible for that invention to be predicted—for it to be announced prior to ten p.m. on 1 March 1650, that a particular man would invent the corkscrew—then the observer who made this prediction would be the first person to announce the invention of the corkscrew. But if he knows about the corkscrew before the 'inventor' has invented it, he, *the observer*, must be the true inventor. These examples suggest that neither creative work nor inventions are in principle predictable.

Yet another argument for the impossibility of prediction I borrow from Popper's essay *Indeterminism in Quantum Physics*.[1] This argument is an adaptation of the 'Tristram Shandy paradox'. Readers will remember that Tristram Shandy tries to write a complete account of his life, but finds it takes more time to describe each event than each event takes to happen. Thus, instead of his autobiography becoming progressively more up to date, it becomes instead more and more hopelessly out of date the longer he works at it and the longer he lives. Tristram Shandy's dilemma illustrates the difficulty Popper is concerned with; a difficulty not of describing the past, but of predicting the future. His point is, broadly speaking, that the material or information necessary for a prediction to be made is unlikely to be complete until a point of time very close to the occurrence of the event or state predicted. In fact, so close will that point of time be that there will be no time for the actual utterance (or writing) of that prediction. Suppose, for example, an event or state at Time 5 is to be predicted; and the prediction is to be given at Time 4. However fast the machinery works in the case of a mechanical prediction, or however fast a man speaks in the case of a human prediction, a statement begun at Time 4 is unlikely to have been completed until Time 5 or even Time 6, when it will be too late to be prediction.

In Popper's essay the 'Tristram Shandy paradox' is one of several points he makes in criticism of the common belief that 'classical physics is determinist and quantum physics indeterminist', and he argues that 'most systems of physics, including classical physics and

[1] *The British Journal for the Philosophy of Science*, vol. 1, nos. 2 and 3 (1950).

quantum physics are indeterministic in perhaps an even more fundamental sense than the one usually ascribed to the indeterminism of
quantum physics'. Popper's method is to examine the properties and
the limitations of what he calls the *predictor*—a classical mechanical
calculating and predicting machine which is so constructed as to
produce permanent records of some kind, capable of being interpreted
as predictions. The result of these considerations leads, he concludes, to
a restitution of the *naive* view of the world—'the view that there are
events which can be predicted, or which are "determined", and other
events which cannot be predicted and are not "determined" '.

§

It is to precisely this conclusion of Popper's that our present enquiry
has led us.[1] In effect, we are closer to the libertarian than we are to the
determinist. That is partly because the theory of the freedom of the
will is not dogmatic, as determinism is. The libertarian theory admits
'a large measure of determinism' in the sense that it admits a large
measure of predictability. Determinism can admit nothing of the
libertarian claim, since it upholds total and comprehensive predictability.

There is nothing sinister in the hospitality which libertarianism
affords to a large measure of predictability, as R. E. Hobart seemed to
think when he said[2] that the freedom of the will was dependent on
determinism. For no intelligent advocate of the freedom of the will
has thought he could dispense with causal explanation altogether
when he has said that motives and choices are not always effects.

Certainly the libertarian cannot be said to deny that actions have
motives or to imply that all actions are capricious. Both Bradley[3] and
Green[4] make this fantastic allegation, and there is an echo in A. J.

---

[1] Professor Popper has asked me to make it clear that I had reached these
conclusions before I read his paper. When that paper appeared in the *British
Journal for the Philosophy of Science* in 1950 I had already written down my own
argument in a thesis I wrote at Oxford. I found in Popper's paper what I believe
to be a substantial reinforcement of my argument; but my argument does not
derive in any way from his, apart from the fact that I have taken the 'Tristram
Shandy' illustration from it.
[2] *Mind* (January 1934), p. 1.
[3] F. H. Bradley, *Ethical Studies* (2nd edn., Oxford, 1927), pp. 9–11.
[4] T. H. Green, *Prolegomena to Ethics* (2nd edn., Oxford, 1884), §6.

Ayer's[1] remark:

> ... if it is not an accident that I choose to do one thing rather than another, then presumably there is some causal explanation of my choice.

Ayer's statement is doubly unfortunate in that it implies (1) that accidents are uncaused (2) that every happening that is not explicable as an effect is an accident. In fact, of course, accidents are *undeliberated*, not uncaused. When an accident happens we always ask: 'What caused it?' Again, people who have said that choices are not effects have usually made it quite clear that they regard choices as the result of deliberation. To say that a choice is the result of deliberation is not to say it is accidental; on the contrary, it is to say that it is *not* accidental.

§

My argument brings me close to the libertarian conclusion, but not quite to it. The traditional libertarian must prove that moral choices and decisions are 'undetermined' or unpredictable by the methods of science. I have shown, I believe, that some human thoughts and activities, and notably *creative* activity, is unpredictable by the methods of science. I have not been able to prove the same of moral choices and decisions. Indeed, modern psychology has abundantly shown that much of the behaviour that is taken as evidence of moral choices and decisions *is* predictable by the methods of science.

For the theory of the freedom of the will to be established positively, it would have to be possible for a man to say 'it was psychologically possible for me to have chosen or decided differently', and to adduce evidence in support of that statement.

That statement is about the past, and, in part at any rate, contrafactual. It refers to a choice or decision that has *not in fact* been made. The crucial question is: how can any contrafactual statement about the past be proved?

It has more than once been demonstrated in recent years that the modern logic of truth functions cannot easily accommodate contrafactual hypothetical statements[2] (e.g. 'If Germany had invaded

---

[1] *Polemic* 5, p. 39.

[2] See articles in *Mind*, by R. M. Chisholm (1946), F. L. Will (1947) and B. J. Diggs (1952); in the *Journal of Philosophy*, by N. Goodman (1947) and H. Weinberg (1950); in *Analysis* by D. F. Pears, S. Hampshire, and A. R. Anderson (1951).

Sweden in 1940, she would soon have overcome any military re-
sistance'). Nevertheless we discuss, dispute or believe a great number of
statements cast in this form, whatever the logicians' embarrassment
with regard to their classification. We give assent to such contrafactual
hypothetical statements because we believe in the truth of certain factual
propositions which are the grounds for their assertion (e.g. 'Sweden's
military resources in 1940 were weak: those of Germany were strong').

The statement 'I could have chosen otherwise' presents not only the
difficulty of classification in logic. There is the difficulty of saying what
empirically verifiable fact constitutes grounds for its assertion. So far as
this psychological possibility of electing between alternatives is
concerned, the testimony of 'introspection' is, as we have seen,
confused.

When I think of the decisions I made yesterday I certainly believe
I could have made different ones. I feel almost as certain about the
decisions I made last year. I am less sure about decisions made five years
ago. When I look back ten or twenty years I see my choices more and
more under the form of determinism. I am increasingly inclined to
think that what I decided then I could not help deciding. Thus so far
as the test of inner feeling goes, the close range seems to favour
libertarianism, the long range determinism. Spinoza said: 'Those . . .
who believe they do anything from the free decision of the mind
dream with their eyes open' (*Ethics*, III, prop. 2n). Experiments with
'post-hypnotic' suggestion provide some support for Spinoza's belief.
For example, a hypnotist might say to a patient: 'Tomorrow at four
o'clock you will remove your shoes.' The following day, long after
he has emerged from the trance, the patient removes his shoes, possibly
in circumstances which render his action seem decidedly eccentric.
The interesting feature of this case is not the action itself, however, but
what the patient says when he is asked why, at that particular time and
place, he removed his shoes. He will not say he felt some strange inner
compulsion. He will say, perhaps, that his shoes looked muddy or felt
damp and that he decided for this or that reason to remove them. We,
who are privy to the hypnotist's command, *know* he did not act from
any such 'free decision of the mind'. His action was caused, and it was
predictable by the methods of science. Nevertheless I think Spinoza is
wrong. From the fact that we are *sometimes* deceived about our motives,
it does not follow that we *always* are.

Priestley, a thoroughgoing determinist, wrote in *The Doctrine of
Philosophical Necessity* in 1782:

A man indeed when he reproaches himself for any particular action in his past conduct may fancy that if he were in the same situation again, he would have acted (or decided) differently. But this is a mere deception; and if he examines himself strictly, and takes in all circumstances, he may be satisfied that, with the same inward disposition of mind and with precisely the same view of things which he had then, and exclusive of all others which he has acquired by reflection since, he would not have acted (or decided) otherwise than he did.

A positive alternative to this view cannot be conclusively established. Such a case requires facts; and the propositions to be proved are contrafactual.

Hence the residual uncertainty as to whether the libertarian case holds good. I have suggested that there the weight of the argument is strongly against determinism. Beyond that it seems to me foolish to expect to move with certainty. Our enquiry has afforded some grounds for belief and some for doubt. Without grounds for doubt the subject would not be philosophy; and without grounds for belief there would be no point in writing.

SUMMARY OF CONTENTS

PART ONE

'Freedom' means the absence of constraints, etc.; but constraints are of many kinds; hence freedoms are of many kinds. The word 'freedom' is incompletely descriptive. To understand what 'freedom' means, we must know what it is freedom *from* or freedom *for*. 'Freedom' has, nevertheless, a fairly constant *emotive* meaning. It is a laudatory word. Many philosophers have tried to make freedom 'positive'. Various utterances on the subject quoted and considered. The doctrine that freedom is a *faculty* criticized. The doctrine that freedom is 'government by reason' examined, together with a refinement of that doctrine which holds that man can be 'forced to be free'. A preliminary criticism of these doctrines of *rational* and *enforceable rational* freedom. Do such theories of freedom rest on a redefinition of freedom? The principles of definition discussed. Lexicographical definition, which reports conventional usage, distinguished from stipulative definition, an acceptable device for eliminating ambiguity. *Faculty* definitions of 'freedom' are lexicographical, but erroneous; *rational* and *enforceable rational* definitions of 'freedom' seem to be neither lexicographical nor useful stipulative definitions. Are they *persuasive* definitions? Or are they not definitions, but disguised value judgments? Persuasive definitions aim at altering the descriptive meaning while retaining the emotive meaning of laudatory words. How do they succeed? How do persuasive definitions of 'freedom' come to persuade? Partly because the notion of being unconstrained seems negative, and there is a demand for what is positive and moral; partly because not everyone likes being unconstrained.

PART TWO

If a liberal is defined as a man who believes in political liberty, the word 'liberal' will vary as the word 'liberty' varies. Since 'liberty' is synonymous with 'freedom', it would be absurd to expect the word 'liberalism' to be uniquely descriptive. There is no one sort of liberalism because there is no one sort of freedom. Even in one language 'liberalism' may have several different meanings. The merits and weaknesses of *English* liberalism discussed. Two important senses of *libéralisme* distinguished, Lockean and *étatiste*; their successes and failures. The connection between liberalism and democracy. Early German liberalism of the *Naturrechts* School swamped by an *étatiste* liberalism imported from France and reinforced with a metaphysical theory of freedom. German liberalism embraces nationalism, and is embraced by imperialism. 'Liberalism', a word alien to American political terminology, used by Parrington to describe various phases of progressive American thought; adopted by Roosevelt to name his politics of the Centre and then by 'Fellow Travellers' for the politics of the Left. 'Liberal' fast becoming a pejorative word in many circles U.S.A.

PART THREE

The problem of reconciling the freedom of the will (1) with the omniscience of God (2) the 'scientific' belief that everything that happens in the universe is predictable in principle. The suggestion that the problem of the freedom of the will is a pseudo-problem examined and refuted. The attempts of philosophers (including Kant, Bergson, Wisdom, Eddington, and Weiss) to solve the problem considered and found wanting. If the will is not free, do ethical judgments become irrelevant and absurd? No, the determinist can give his own analysis of ethical judgments. But it is one which is in some respects at variance with the common sense. The libertarian can give a more convincing analysis. The problem restated. Are all human choices and actions predictable in principle? Determinism affirms this; libertarianism denies it. Nature and scope of prediction discussed, its limitations illustrated. Arguments *against* determinism found most telling.

FURTHER READING

ADLER, MORTIMER J. *The Idea of Freedom*, 2 vols., 1961.

AGGOGNANO, N. 'Contemporary Science and Freedom', *Review of Metaphysics*, March 1952.

ANSHEN, RUTH N., ed. *Freedom, Its Meaning*, 1940.

ARENDT, H. 'Freiheit und Politik', *Die Neue Rundschau*, 1958.

ARON, RAYMOND. *Essai sur la liberté*, Paris 1965.

BAY, CHRISTIAN. *The Structure of Freedom*, 1958.

BAYLIS, C. A. 'Rational Preferences, Determinism, and Moral Obligation', *Journal of Philosophy*, February 1950.

BENN, S. and PETERS, R. S. *Social Principles and the Democratic State*, 1960.

BERGSON, H. *Time and Free Will*, trans. F. L. Pogson, 1950.

BERLIN, I. *Two Concepts of Liberty* (Inaugural Lecture), 1958.

—— *Historical Inevitability*, 1955.

BRUNSCHVICG, LÉON. *Nature et Liberté*, Paris 1921.

BRYSON, LYMAN, ed. *Freedom and Authority in Our Time*, 1953.

CAMPBELL, C. A. *In Defence of Free Will*, 1938.

—— 'Is Free Will a Pseudo-Problem?' *Mind*, October 1951.

CAMUS, A. *The Rebel*, 1954.

CASSINELLI, C. W. *The Politics of Freedom*, 1960.

CASSIRER, E. *Determinism and Indeterminism in Modern Physics*, 1956.

CHRISTOF, D. *Recherche de la liberté*, Paris 1957.

COKER, F. W. 'Some present-day critics of Liberalism', *American Political Science Review*, March 1953.

CRANSTON, M. *What are Human Rights?*, 1962.

—— 'Freedom, discipline and bondage', *Philosophy*, April 1948.

DELLA VOLPE, G. *La libertá communista*, Messina, 1946.

DEVLIN, LORD. *The Enforcement of Morals*, 1964.

DEUTSCH, KARL W. 'The value of freedom', *The American Scholar*, 1948.

EBERSOLE, F. B. 'Free choice and the demands of morals', *Mind*, April 1952.

ENTRÈVES, A. P. D'. 'Obeying whom?', *Political Studies*, 1965.

EWING, A. C. 'Indeterminism', *Review of Metaphysics*, December 1951.

FARRER, A. *The Freedom of the Will*, 1958.

FLEW, A. 'Determinism', *The Rationalist Annual*, 1953.

FOOT, PHILIPPA. 'Free will as involving determinism', *The Philosophical Review*, October 1957.

FRIEDRICH, C. J. *Constitutional Government and Democracy*, 1961.

—— *Man and His Government*, 1963.

——, ed. *Liberty* (Nomos Series IV), 1962.

FROMM, ERICH. *The Fear of Freedom*, 1941.

GALLOP, D. 'On being determined', *Mind*, April 1962.

GALLIE, W. B. *Free Will and Determinism Yet Again* (Inaugural Lecture), 1957.

GELLNER, E. 'Determinism and validity', *The Rationalist Annual*, 1955.

GRINDEL, CARL W., ed. *The Concept of Freedom*, 1955.

HAMPSHIRE, STUART. *Freedom of the Individual*, 1965.

HARDIE, W. R. F. 'My own free will', *Philosophy*, January 1957.

HARE, R. M. *Freedom and Reason*, 1963.

HARSHORNE, CHARLES. 'Freedom requires determinism', *Journal of Philosophy*, September 1958.

HART, H. L. A. *The Concept of Law*, 1961.

HARTNACK, J. 'Free will and decision', *Mind*, July 1953.

HARTZ, L. *The Liberal Tradition in America*, 1960.

HAYEK, F. A. VON. *The Constitution of Liberty*, 1960.

HERBST, P. 'Freedom and prediction', *Mind*, January 1957.

HIPPOLYTE, J. 'La liberté chez J.-P. Sartre', *Mercure de France*, July 1951.

HOOK, SIDNEY, ed. *Determinism and Freedom*, 1958.

JASPERS, K. 'Freedom and authority', *Diogenes*, Winter 1953.

JOUVENEL, B. DE. *Power*, 1948.

—— *Sovereignty*, 1957.

—— 'A discussion of freedom', *Cambridge Journal*, 1953.

KAUFMAN, ARNOLD S. 'Practical decision', *Mind*, January 1966.

KNIGHT, FRANK H. *Freedom and Reform*, 1947.

KRIEGER, L. *The German Idea of Freedom*, 1950.

LECKE, W. E. H. *Democracy and Liberty*, 1896.

MABBOTT, J. D. 'Free will and punishment', in *Contemporary British Philosophy*, ed. H. D. Lewis, 1956.

MCCLOSKEY, H. J. 'A critique of the ideals of liberty', *Mind*, October 1965.

MACINTYRE, A. C. 'Determinism', *Mind*, January 1957.

MACKAY, D. M. 'On the logical indeterminacy of a free choice', *Mind*, January 1960.

MCKEON, RICHARD. *Freedom and History*, 1952.

MACLAGAN, W. G., *et al.* 'The Freedom of the will', *Proceedings of the Aristotelian Society*, suppl. vol. xxv, 1951.

MANDELBAUM, M. 'Determinism and moral responsibility', *Ethics*, April 1960.

MATSON, WALLACE I. 'On the irrelevance of free-will', *Mind*, October 1956.

MAYO, B. 'The open future', *Mind*, January 1962.

MILL, J. S. *On Liberty*, 1859; ed. R. B. MacCallum, 1846.

MORRIS, H., ed. *Freedom and Responsibility*, 1961.

MULLER, A. J. *Issues of Freedom*, 1960.

NEUMANN, FRANZ. *The Democratic and the Authoritarian State*, 1957.

NOWELL-SMITH, P. H. *Ethics*, 1954.

—— 'Determinists and Libertarians', *Mind*, July 1954.

—— 'Free will and moral responsibility', *Mind*, January 1948.

OAKESHOTT, M. *Rationalism in Politics*, 1962.

O'CONNOR, D. J. 'Possibility and choice', *Proceedings of the Aristotelian Society*, 1960.

OPPENHEIM, FELIX E. *Dimensions of Freedom*, 1961.

PAPANOUTSOS, E. P. 'Freedom and Causality', *Philosophy*, July 1959.

PENNOCK, J. ROLAND. *Liberal Democracy*, 1950.

PLAMENATZ, J. *Consent, Freedom and Political Obligation*, 1938.

POLANYI, M. *The Logic of Liberty*, 1951.

POPPER, KARL R. 'Indeterminism in Quantum physics', *The British Journal of the Philosophy of Science*, August and November 1950.

—— *The Poverty of Historicism*, 1957.

—— *Conjectures and Refutations*, 1963.

RAPHAEL, D. D. 'Law and morals', *Philosophical Quarterly*, 1954.

——, ed. *Human Rights and Political Theory*, 1967.

RICOEUR, P. *Philosophie de la volonté*, Paris, 1950.

SALVADORI, MASSIMO. *Liberty and Progress*, 1957.

—— *Locke and Liberty*, 1959.

SARTRE, J.-P. *Being and Nothingness*, trans. Hazel Barnes, 1956.

SCALAN, JAMES P. 'J. S. Mill and the definition of Freedom', *Ethics*, 1958.

SCOTT, R. J. 'Liberty, license and not being free', *Political Studies*, June 1956.

SKINNER, R. C. 'Freedom of choice', *Mind*, October 1963.

SMART, J. J. C. 'Free will, praise and blame', *Mind*, July 1961.

STEPHEN, J. FITZJAMES. *Liberty, Equality, Fraternity*, 1863.

TINET, CARL. 'Can the will be caused?' *Philosophical Review*, 1962.

UNESCO. *Enquête sur la liberté*, Paris, 1953.

VIVIAN, F. *Human Freedom and Responsibility*, 1964.

WALKER, P. C. GORDON. *Restatement of Liberty*, 1951.

WEIL, SIMONE. *Oppression and Liberty*, 1958.

WEINSTEIN, W. L. 'The concept of liberty', *Political Studies*, 1965.

WEISS, PAUL. *Man's Freedom*, 1950.

WILSON, J. 'Freedom and compulsion', *Mind*, July 1961.

INDEX OF PROPER NAMES

Acton, Lord, 6, 43
Albertus Magnus, 82, 83
Althusius, J., 64
Aquinas, St. Thomas, 82, 83
Aristotle, 5, 18, 20, 35, 81 100, 110
Auden, W. H., 42
Augustine, St., 81, 82
Ayer, A. J., 39, 40, 87–9, 91, 110, 120

Balfour, A. J., 59
Barker, Sir E., 21, 76
Baumgarten, A. G., 18
Beck, Rt. Rev. G. A., 36
Berdeyaev, N., 35, 42
Bergson, G., 98–100
Bilfinger, G. B., 18
Bismarck, Prince O., 68
Boethius, 81
Bolsec, H. H., 84
Bonnet, C., 17
Bosanquet, B., 18, 21, 23
Bowen, F., 90
Bradley, F. H., 18, 119
Braithwaite, R. B., 104
Brandeis, Judge, 73
Buber, M., 31–2, 42
Butler, Bishop, 18
Byron, Lord, 8

Calvin, J., 83, 84
Campbell, C. A., 94
Camus, A., 42
Charles I, 9, 57

Chesterton, G. K., 56
Cohen, H., 17, 27
Coleridge, S. T., 38–9
Commager, H. S., 71, 74, 75
Constant, B., 61
Copleston, F., 82

Eddington, Sir A., 101–3, 104
Eliot, George, 111
Eliot, T. S., 33
Empson, W., 21
Engels, F., 17
Erasmus, 83

Faguet, E., 62–3
Forster, E. M., 26, 51, 75
Friedrich, Wilhelm IV, 66, 68
Fromm, E., 36

Garnett, C., 89
Gide, A., 35, 41–2
Goddard, Lord, 112
Gordon Walker, P., 39
Grandvilliers, J. de, 63, 69
Greeley, H., 70
Green, T. H., 119
Grene, M., 41
Grotius, H., 64, 66
Guizot, F., 62

Hallowell, J. H., 47, 50, 67
Hampshire, S. N., 111
Hartland-Swann, J. J., 113
Hegel, G., 17, 21, 27, 39
Heidegger, M., 3, 5, 17, 27, 41

Hobart, R. E., 119
Hobbes, T., 15, 17, 28, 39, 48, 52, 54, 84, 85, 86
Hobhouse, L. T., 54
Holloway, C. J., 24
Hooker, T., 72
Housman, A. E., 33
Humboldt, W. von, 64
Hume, D., 17, 39, 86, 87, 92
Huxley, A., 34

James I, 57
Jefferson, T., 62
Johnson, S., 104

Kant, I., 17, 20, 38, 95-7, 99
Keats, J., 117
Keynes, Maynard, 54
Kierkegaard, S., 42
Kraus, C. J., 65

Lalande, A., 29
Lange, J., 114
Laski, H., 47
Leibniz, G.W., 17
Lewis, J., 42
Lincoln, A., 9
Locke, J., 17, 27, 47, 50, 56, 59, 60, 62, 63, 64, 85, 86, 93
Louis, XIV, 58
Louis Philippe, 62, 68
Luther, M., 83

Machiavelli, N., 54
Mann, T., 22
Marcel, G., 42
Maritain, Jacques, 64
Martin, K., 93
Marx, K., 39
Mary II, 62

Matthiessen, F. O., 71, 74, 77
Mill, J. S., 50, 54-5, 94
Milton, J., 12, 18, 20, 56
Montesquieu, Baron de, 18
Moore, G. E., 89
Mortimer, R., 71

Newman, W. L., 21
Nowell-Smith, P., 91-4, 107-9

O'Connor, D. J., 90
Orwell, G., 34

Parrington, V. L., 71-5
Paton, H. J., 31, 98
Paulsen, J., 17
Peirce, C. S., 37
Peters, R. S., 43
Plato, 66
Polanyi, M., 39
Popper, K. R., 118-19
Potter, S., 115
Priestley, J., 121
Pufendorf, S., 64

Read, Sir H., 31, 32, 42
Richards, I. A., 12-15
Robinson, R., 25, 27
Roosevelt, F. D., 10
Rousseau, J. J., 6, 18, 21, 29, 73
Ruggiero, G. de, 48, 66, 67
Runes, D. D., 29
Ryle, G., 97, 114-15

St. Exupéry, A. de, 35
Sartre, J. P., 41, 91
Schelling, F. W. J., 17, 27
Schlick, M., 93
Scotus, Duns, 17
Shakespeare, W., 16, 70

Sidgwick, H., 106
Skeat, W., 70
Smith, A., 65
Smith, Helen, 101
Southey, R., 48
Spinoza, B., 17, 18, 21, 38, 121
Stebbing, S., 101-3
Stevenson, C. L., 13-15, 33, 75, 89-90, 107

Tocqueville, A. de, 62
Tolstoi, Count, 33
Tracy, D. de, 18
Trilling, L., 71

Valéry, P., 25, 33
Voltaire, F. de 18

Watterson, H., 70
Weiss, P., 103-5
Wesley, J., 56
William III, 62
Williams, R., 72
Wirszubski, C., 8
Wisdom, J., 101
Wittgenstein, L., 12, 101
Wolf, C., 18
Woolf, V., 24